CONTENTS

CONQUERING
BULLIES

It's a jungle in here!

27 Game-Oriented Guidance Lessons
For Grades 2-5

12 Story-Based Guidance Lessons
For Grades K-2

WRITTEN BY
Marianne Vandawalker

ILLUSTRATED BY
Harry Norcross

Conquering Bullies

10-DIGIT ISBN: 1-57543-136-X   13-DIGIT ISBN: 978-1-57543-136-9

COPYRIGHT © 2005 MAR*CO PRODUCTS, INC.
Published by mar*co products, inc.
1443 Old York Road
Warminster, PA 18974
1-800-448-2197
www.marcoproducts.com

Cover photo by Cheryl Kemper-Starner

PRINTED IN THE U.S.A.

PAPER JUNGLE ANIMAL HATS 197

ABOUT THE AUTHOR 256

INTRODUCTION

Bullying is one of the most critical social issues facing educators. *Conquering Bullies* was written to help young people develop and practice skills that will enable them to deal effectively with people exhibiting bullying behaviors.

Bullies live in a narrow-minded world with little insight into the problems they cause. The negative behavior patterns that characterize a bully are:

- A low emotional I.Q. Bullies often lack empathy or sympathy for others.
- The lack of the desire to solve problems.
- An overwhelming desire to win.

These behaviors can include inflicting both physical and emotional harm on others. For example, bullying can cause the targeted individual to become sad, think about or attempt suicide, exhibit low self-esteem, and suffer from stress-related disorders.

Positive action can conquer this type of negativity. But positive action will come only through the leadership of responsible, caring adults, such as school administrators, faculty members, and parents. A safe, well-monitored, planned environment can eliminate many of the problems bullies cause. But a structured environment alone will not work if students do not have the confidence to believe they can deal with bullies. *Conquering Bullies* presents strategies students can use to gain this confidence.

HOW TO USE THE PROGRAM

Conquering Bullies uses stories, games, role-playing, and songs to teach important bullying-prevention skills. Written to the tunes of familiar children's songs, the songs bring the characteristics of bullies out into the open in a non-threatening way. They are included in each lesson as an optional feature for leaders who feel comfortable with music and feel they are appropriate for the children to whom the lesson is being presented. Role-playing provides students with a chance to act out, rather than merely talk about, ways to solve problems effectively. Many students find role-playing to be a fun and instructive learning experience. It also gives adults the opportunity to provide students with *supervised* practice in dealing with "real-life" problem situations.

Although the *Jungle Animal Hats* are an integral part of the program, and children will enjoy wearing them, they are not essential. Leaders should construct the 12 hats before beginning the program. Each hat represents an animal which, in turn, represents a bullying-type behavior. Children quickly learn to identify bullying behaviors as they relate these actions to the various animals. It is important for leaders to periodically remind the children that although they are relating bullying behaviors to jungle animals, these animals do not really exhibit these behaviors.

The program's stories, games, and role-plays give students time to think, share, plan, and practice before having to confront a bully. These activities also give confidence to children already involved in a bullying situation. They help children relate to bullying situations and realize that they can be bold and successful.

Conquering Bullies can be used for classroom guidance or adapted for small-group skill development. The stories, games, and role-plays build confidence and encourage problem-solving.

SUMMARY

Conquering Bullies creates a forum for open communication between youngsters and adults, introducing dialogue on a subject that is often ignored. Students and adults often call it *tattling* on someone if anyone complains about being the target of another person's pattern of negative behaviors. But bullies must be *exposed* instead of *protected*.

Being targeted by a bully can leave a person feeling worthless and helpless. *Conquering Bullies* is designed to prepare and validate individuals as they "take up" for themselves.

Have fun with *Conquering Bullies*, but remember that this important issue will not be resolved until we all get involved.

REPRODUCIBLE PAGES

All of the program's reproducible activity sheets and game cards are included in the back of this book.

EVALUATING THE PROGRAM

When implementing a curriculum, it is important to measure the growth students have made. By administering pre- and post-tests, the facilitator can determine which skills the students have learned and mastered and which, if any, need to be reinforced for an individual or the entire class. Monitoring a program also demonstrates that the facilitator is evaluating his/her own classroom performance.

A *Pre/Post-Test Evaluation* is included in the *Conquering Bullies* program (page 8). You may reproduce this test for your students. Administer the test prior to starting the program and at the conclusion of the lessons. The answers are:

- **True/False:** 1. T, 2. F, 3. T, 4. T, 5. T, 6. F, 7. F, 8. F, 9. T, 10. T

- **Bullying Behaviors:** The following behaviors should be circled: name-calling, threatening, bossiness, harassment, excluding, gossiping, putting others down, snobbishness, aggressiveness, lying, rudeness.

- **Bullying-Diffusion Techniques:** The following techniques should be circled: getting support from friends; joking with the bully; agreeing with the bully if he/she is right; ignoring the bully; confronting the bully; being assertive; making a deal with the bully; acting surprised; complimenting the bully; distracting the bully.

CONQUERING BULLIES
PRE/POST-TEST EVALUATION

NAME _____ DATE _____

True or False. Circle the correct answer.

1.	Bullies want everyone and everything to be just like they are.	T	F
2.	A gossip is someone who doesn't mean to hurt other people.	T	F
3.	A person who leaves others out of a game is a hurtful bully.	T	F
4.	Bullies call others mean or nasty names.	T	F
5.	When a bully threatens you, you could try changing the subject.	T	F
6.	A bossy person is not a bully.	T	F
7.	A threatening bully might say, "You are the worst ball player."	T	F
8.	Confronting a threatening bully is a good technique.	T	F
9.	A bully is someone who blames others for his/her actions.	T	F
10.	Bullies act as if they are better than others.	T	F

Circle the behaviors below that bullies use toward other people:

Name-calling	Threatening
Helpfulness	Sportsmanship
Bossiness	Honesty
Harassment	Excluding
Putting Others Down	Gossiping
Snobbishness	Aggressiveness
Lying	Trustworthiness
Respect	Rudeness

Circle the techniques that are effective when a person is the victim of bullying.

Getting support from friends

Telling no one

Joking with the bully

Finding a way to get back at the bully

Yelling

Agreeing with the bully if he/she is right

Ignoring the bully

Giving the bully whatever he/she wants

Confronting the bully

Being assertive

Making a deal with the bully

Organizing a bullying gang of your own

Acting surprised

Complimenting the bully

Distracting the bully

8

GUIDANCE LESSONS

RECOGNIZING BULLIES

Six games for grades 2-5 to help students
recognize the different types of bullies

 # BULLY'S WORLD

Purpose:

To make students aware that bullies live in a small-minded world, not a tolerant world

Grade Levels: 2-5

Materials Needed:

For The Leader:

☐ Copy of *Bully World Categories* (page 144)
☐ Copy of *Bully World Cards* (pages 145-147)
☐ Chalkboard and chalk

Pre-Lesson Preparation:

Make a copy of the *Bully World Categories* and the *Bully World Cards.* Cut apart the *Bully World Cards* and laminate them for durability.

Lesson:

Optional: If the songs are part of your presentation, write the following words on the chalkboard:

THERE WAS A BULLY

There was a boy who was so mean,
And Bully was his name—o.
B-U-L-L-Y, B-U-L-L-Y, B-U-L-L-Y,
And Bully was his name—o.

There was a girl who was so mean,
And Bully was her name—o.
B-U-L-L-Y, B-U-L-L-Y, B-U-L-L-Y,
And Bully was her name—o.

Then tell the children:

> **Today we will be learning about bullies. We are going to begin by learning a song. The name of the song is _There Was A Bully_. We will sing it to the tune of _Bingo_. How many of you have heard or know that song? (Pause for responses.) Can anyone sing one verse for us?** (Allow one or more students to sing a verse of _Bingo_.)

Help the students with any new words in _There Was A Bully_. Practice the words of the new song, line by line, with the class. Have the students repeat each line to you. Then have the students sing the song.

Introduce or continue the lesson by telling the students:

> **A _bully_ is someone who mistreats others either physically, by trying to hurt them, or verbally, by trying to hurt their feelings. A bully sends a lot of negative (bad) messages, such as pushing you or calling you names, instead of positive (good) messages, such as playing nicely or complimenting you.**
>
> **You may wonder why anyone would act this way. It's hard to imagine, but some people feel safer when everyone and everything is just like them. But it is our differences that make us unique and special. In the _Real World_, people like different things and do different things. _Bully World_ is a small-minded world. Bullies believe everyone should be just like they are and do everything just the way they do. As long as bullies can live in their small-minded world, they feel safe.**

Game Procedure:

Introduce the game by saying:

> **Today we are going to play a game called _Bully World_. I will hand out one card to each of you. Read it silently and keep what it says a secret. I will walk past all of your desks as you read your cards. If you need help with reading or understanding your card, hold it out as I pass your desk. I will help you.**

Distribute the _Bully World Cards_.

After you are sure everyone understands what is written on the cards, say:

> **I am going to divide the room into two sides. The left side of the room is _Bully World_.** (Point to the left side of the room.) **The right side of the room is _Real World_.** (Point to the right side of the room.) **I am going to read a list of categories. If your card has something to do with the category I read, leave your seat and walk either to the _Bully World_ or the _Real World_. If your card says you are different**

from the bully, walk to the right side of the room—*Real World*. If your card says you are the same as the bully, walk to the left side of the room—*Bully World.* For example, if I say, "color of hair," and your card has something to do with hair color, decide if the words on your card make you the same as or different from the bully. After you have made your decision, move to either the right or left side of the room.

If you land in *Real World*, you are different from the bully and the bully might pick on you. After we finish category each round, we will discuss how you feel about the sentence on your *Bully World Card* and whether you deserve to be picked on because you were different from the bully.

Do not move from your seats until after I have finished reading the category and you hear me say, "Move." After everyone has moved to either *Bully World* on the left side of the room or *Real World* on the right, I will say, "Take your seats." Then you will sit down and we will discuss what happened.

Are there any questions?

One at a time, read aloud each of the *Bully World Categories*. After reading each category, give the students time to think. Then say, "Move." After everyone in the class has moved to either *Bully World* or *Real World,* let the students look around at where they are. Then say, "Take your seats."

Follow-Up:

At the conclusion of the activity, ask the students the following questions:

How would you feel if you were picked on because of your skin color, sports ability, eyesight, classroom behavior, etc.?

Would you deserve to be picked on for these type of reasons? Why or why not?

 # WALK ON THE WILD SIDE

Purpose:

To make students aware of the different ways a person might bully someone

Grade Levels: 2-5

Materials Needed:

For The Leader:

☐ *Jungle Animal Hats* (4 hats for grades K-1, 8 hats for grades 2-3, and all 12 hats for grades 4-6, pages 197-255)
☐ Copy of *Jungle Animal Cards* (pages 149-150)
☐ Chalkboard and chalk (optional)
☐ Cassette and cassette player or CD and CD player for lively music (optional)

For Each Student:

☐ Copy of *Old MacDonald Had A School* (optional, page 148)

Pre-Lesson Preparation:

Select the *Jungle Animal Hats* to be used in the lesson and select the correlating *Jungle Animal Cards.* Make each hat according to its directions.

Make a copy of the *Jungle Animal Cards*. Cut apart the cards and laminate them for durability.

If you are using the *Old MacDonald Had A School* song, make a copy for each student.

Lesson:

Optional: If the songs are part of your presentation, distribute *Old MacDonald Had A School* to each student.

Then say:

> **Today we will be learning about bullies. We are going to begin this lesson by learning a song. The name of the song is *Old MacDonald Had A School*. We will sing it to the tune of *Old MacDonald Had A Farm*. How many of you have heard or know that song?** (Pause for responses.) **Can anyone sing one verse for us?** (Allow one or more students to sing a verse of *Old MacDonald Had A Farm*.)

Help the students with any new words in *Old MacDonald Had A School*. Practice the words of the new song, line by line, with the class. Have the students repeat each line to you. Then have the students sing the song.

Introduce or continue the lesson by asking the students:

> **Who can tell me some ways that bullies act toward other kids?** (Allow time for answers and, if desired, write them on the chalkboard. Answers should include: Bullies leave others out of playing, call names, yell at others, put others down by making fun of them or not listening to them, accuse others of doing things that they do themselves, never apologize and mean it, threaten to hurt others, gossip, and any other appropriate answer. Different age groups will suggest a different number of bullying characteristics.)

Game Procedure:

Introduce the game by saying:

> **Today we are going to take a *walk on the wild side* into the jungle. I have hats shaped like some of the jungle animals that we might meet on our walk. Each jungle animal hat represents a type of bully that we might have in our school or that you might have in your neighborhood.**

As you place the *Jungle Animal Hats* on the floor in a circle, explain or review what type of bully each hat represents. Then say:

> **The hats are in a circle. In a few minutes, I will ask some of you to walk up and stand beside a hat. When I do, please do not step on the hats. However, first I want to explain what we will be doing in our *walk on the wild side*.**

> **Our *walk on the wild side* is a game in which everyone participating walks around the circle in the same direction while music plays/we clap our hands. When the music stops, each person must stop walking.**

When I start the music/hand-clapping, the students chosen to walk on the outside of the circle will begin walking around the circle in a clockwise direction. (If you are using hand-clapping, have the students clap along with you.) **When the music/hand-clapping stops, I will take a *Jungle Animal Card* from the deck. The name of one of the animals is printed on each card. If someone in the circle is standing beside the hat that represents the animal whose name I call, he or she then gets to put on the hat and pretend to be that kind of bully.**

I will draw a card and give it to the *bully*. The *bully* should choose one of the two behaviors printed on each card, walk to someone sitting in the classroom, then act out the chosen behavior. I will whisper to you how the animal on the card is supposed to behave if you need me to do so. For example, if you get a hippo card, this animal stands for the type of bully that calls names. Please remember this is only role-playing. No one should try to intentionally hurt another person's feelings and no touching is allowed.

After the *bully* has role-played the behavior, the person who is seated must tell why the jungle animal's behavior is an example of bullying. For example, the person might say, "The bully calls names."

Of course, acting like a bully once does not make anyone a bully. A person would have to behave this way to others repeatedly before we could be sure that his or her actions are those of a true bully.

If the person sitting down correctly names the bullying behavior, he or she may come up to the circle for the next round. (*Note:* The leader could also let the person who answers correctly choose other students to come to the front circle to replace the students who are currently standing there.)

Choose the students to walk around the outside of the circle and begin the first round of the game. Continue playing the game until the allotted time has elapsed or until you are satisfied that the students have begun to recognize some ways that bullies might behave.

Follow-Up:

At the conclusion of the activity, ask the students the following questions:

Without using any names, which of the bullies in our lesson today have you been around before?

How do you feel when a bully (finish the question by selecting one or more of the bully characteristics identified on the *Jungle Animal Hats*)**?**

 # SPOT THE BULLY

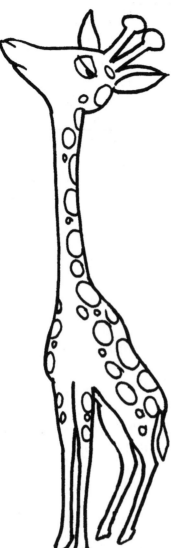

Purpose:

To help students "spot" negative words and behavior

Grade Levels: 2-5

Materials Needed:

For The Leader:

☐ 10 *Jungle Animal Hats* (pages 197-255)
☐ Copy of *Spot The Bully Situation List* (pages 152-153)
☐ Copy of *Spot The Bully Cards* (pages 154-155)
☐ Large piece of black construction paper
☐ Compass or large coffee can
☐ Chalk
☐ Scissors

For Each Student:

☐ Copy of *The Bully In The School* song (optional, page 151)

Pre-Lesson Preparation:

If not constructed previously, make each of the 10 *Jungle Animal Hats,* omitting the monkey and the zebra, according to its directions.

Make a copy of the *Spot The Bully Situation List* and the *Spot The Bully Cards.* Cut apart the *Spot The Bully Cards* and laminate them for durability.

Using the bottom of the large coffee can or compass, draw three circles on the black construction paper. Cut the circles out. Using chalk, number the circles 1, 2, and 3. Laminate them for durability.

If you are using *The Bully In The School* song, Make a copy for each student.

Lesson:

Optional: If the songs are part of your presentation, distribute *The Bully In The School* to each student. Then say:

> **Today we will begin our lesson by learning a song about a bully. It is called *The Bully In The School* and it is sung to the tune of *The Farmer In The Dell*. How many of you have heard or know that song?** (Pause for responses.) **Can anyone sing one verse for us?** (Allow one or more students to sing a verse of *The Farmer In The Dell*.)

Help the students with any new words in *The Bully In The School*. Practice the words of the new song, line by line, with the class. Have the students repeat each line to you. Then have the students sing the song.

Introduce or continue the lesson by saying:

> **Today we are going to recognize things that bullies say and do. What are some things that bullies might say?** (Pause for students' answers. Bullies might call names, yell, boss people around, etc.) **When someone says something in a bullying manner, it is called *verbal abuse* or *verbal mistreatment of others*.**
>
> **What are some examples of things that bullies might do?** (Pause for responses. Bullies might shove, push, kick, cut ahead of others in line, etc.) **When someone does something in a bullying manner, it is called *physical abuse* or *physical mistreatment of others*.**

Game Procedure:

Show the students the cards and the three black spots. Then explain the game by saying:

> **I will choose three volunteers to come to the front of the room to pretend to be *bullies*. Who would like to volunteer?** (Choose three volunteers and ask them to come to the front of the room.) **Thank you. Please stand in a line an arm's length apart. Do not turn your backs to the class.**
>
> **I will now choose three more volunteers to come to the front of the room. I will give each of these students a black circle or *spot* with a number on it. Who would like to volunteer?** (Choose three volunteers who will *Spot The Bully* and ask them to come to the front of the room.) **I would like the three *spotters* to stand in a line facing the three *bullies*.** (There should be about six feet between the two lines of students. The two lines should be parallel to each other with their sides to the class. Neither the *bullies* nor the *spotters* should have their backs to the class. Allow time for the players to get into position.)

Continue explaining the game by saying:

I will give each *bully* a *Spot The Bully Card*. One card will have a type of bullying response printed on it. The other two cards will say: *You are not a bully!* Then I will read the first situation aloud. The three *bullies* will each respond to the situation, but only the student holding the card with a *type of bullying response* printed on it will respond like a bully. The two students holding *You are not a bully!* cards will give non-bully-like answers. The *bully* should respond with one of the possible bullying responses written on the card. For example, if the situation states: "It's my turn to use the computer," and the card says: *Threatening*, the *bully* might say, "I am going to use the computer and if you don't like it, you can meet me after school and we'll settle it then." This would be a threatening remark. However, the other two players will say something like: "OK, let me know when you're finished," or "Right. Give me just a minute to finish what I'm doing." In order not to give away the secret, each *bully* must pretend to read a card before responding.

After hearing the three responses, the *spotters* will toss their *spots* as you would throw a Frisbee toward the feet of the true *bully*. The *spotter* whose *spot* lands closest to the true *bully* may stay up in front for another turn. The other *spotters* should return to their seats. I will then choose two new people to replace those *spotters*.

A *spotter* may win only three rounds. After being correct three times, he or she may choose a replacement *spotter* from the group. We will applaud the retiring *spotter*.

After each round, I will ask the group what type of bully the *spotters* spotted. The person with the correct answer selects the hat that corresponds to the bully spotted and wears it to remind the class of that type of bullying. That person will also be one of the new *spotters*.

Begin the game. After each round, collect the *Spot The Bully Cards*. Select new *bullies* and *spotters*. Give these students the cards appropriate for the situation you are reading aloud. Then play another round.

Follow-Up:

At the conclusion of the activity, ask the students the following questions:

What helped you *spot the bully*?

Without using any names, tell me what type of bully you have been around.

BULLY BOPPER

Purpose:

To help students recognize verbal abuse

Grade Levels: 2-5

Materials Needed:

For The Leader:

- ☐ *Jungle Animal Hats* (pages 197-255)
- ☐ Copy of *Bully Bopper List* (page 156)
- ☐ Chalkboard and chalk (if you are using the song)
- ☐ 2 balloons of different colors
- ☐ Newspaper

Pre-Lesson Preparation:

If not constructed previously, make each *Jungle Animal Hat* according to its directions.

Make a copy of the *Bully Bopper List.*

Blow up two balloons.

Roll the newspaper for "bopping."

Lesson:

Optional: Review some of the previously taught bully songs. If the songs are part of this presentation, write the following words on the chalkboard:

BULLY IS FALLING DOWN

Bully girl is falling down,
Falling down, falling down.
Bully girl is falling down,
My fair lady.

Bully boy is falling down,
Falling down, falling down.
Bully boy is falling down,
My fair laddie.

Then say:

> Today we will learn the song *Bully Is Falling Down* and we will sing it to the tune
> of *London Bridge Is Falling Down.* How many of you have heard or know that
> song? (Pause for responses.) Can anyone sing one verse for us? (Allow one or
> more students to sing a verse of *London Bridge Is Falling Down.*)

Help the students with any new words in *Bully Is Falling Down.* Practice the words of the new
song, line by line, with the class. Have the students repeat each line to you. Then have the
students sing the song.

Introduce or continue the lesson by saying:

> Bullies might call you names, put you down by saying something that leaves you
> feeling unimportant, or laugh at you. This is called *verbal abuse.* You need to be
> alert and recognize this kind of abuse and you need to remember that *negative
> talk* is *verbal abuse.*

Game Procedure:

Explain or review what type of bully each hat represents. Then introduce the game by saying:

> I am going to have two of you come to the front of the room. (If the students can
> read, choose three students.) One of you will toss two balloons of different colors
> into the air. The (<u>NAME THE COLOR</u>) balloon represents *negative talk*—what a bully
> would say. The (<u>NAME THE COLOR</u>) balloon represents *positive talk*—what a kind
> and caring person would say.
>
> The other person is the *bully bopper.* That person is to hit the balloon that stands
> for the type of statement I will read aloud. (*Note:* If a third student is used, he/she
> can read the statements.)
>
> Whenever a person *bops* a *negative talk* balloon, I will ask for volunteers to
> come to the front of the room and choose the hat that represents the verbal
> abuse just heard.
>
> Each time the wrong color of balloon is *bopped* or after three consecutive cor-
> rect *bops*, I will choose a new balloon tosser and a new *bully bopper.*

If a *bully bopper* is retired after three correct answers, we will applaud his or her efforts.

Select the first players and begin playing the game.

Follow-Up:

At the conclusion of the activity, have the students answer the following:

What helped you recognize the negative bully statements?

Without using any names, tell if you have ever heard anyone make some of these negative bullying statements and what happened because of what he or she said.

BULLY SPY

Purpose:

To help students recognize various types of bullies

Grade Levels: 2-5

Materials Needed:

For The Leader:

☐ *Jungle Animal Hats* (pages 197-255)
☐ Copy of *Jungle Animal Cards* (pages 149-150)
☐ Magnifying glass (optional)

For Each Student:

☐ Copy of the song *If Bully* (optional, page 157)

Pre-Lesson Preparation:

If not constructed previously, make each *Jungle Animal Hat* according to its directions.

Make a copy of the *Jungle Animal Cards*. Cut apart the cards and laminate them for durability.

If your are using the song, make a copy for each student.

Lesson:

Optional: If the songs are part of your presentation, distribute *If Bully* to each student. (*Note:* If the *Zany Zebra* lesson (page 71) has already been presented, the students will be familiar with the song.)

Then say:

> **Before we begin, let's review some of the bully songs that we have learned.** (Have a student lead the singing or lead the singing yourself.) **Today we have a new bully song (are going to sing a bully song we learned before) called *If Bully*. It is**

sung to the tune of *If You're Happy And You Know It.* **How many of you have heard or know that song?** (Pause for responses.) **Can anyone sing one verse for us?** (Allow one or more students to sing a verse from *If You're Happy And You Know It.*)

Help the students with any new words in *If Bully.* Practice the words of the new song, line by line, with the class. Have the students repeat each line to you. Then have the students sing the song.

Game Procedure:

Explain or review what type of bully each hat represents. Then introduce or continue the lesson by explaining the game procedure. Say:

Today we are going to practice being *spies* and finding *bullies*. As we practice recognizing a bully, you will need to lay your head down on your arms on your desk and cover your eyes. I will secretly choose six people. Each person tapped on the head will be a *secret bully*.

Anyone who has *not* been tapped on the head to be a *bully* may volunteer to be a *bully spy* and try to discover the identity of the six *secret bullies*. We will have six *bully spies*.

The first *bully spy* will take a *Jungle Animal Card.* (Hold up the magnifying glass if one is being used.) **The card will name a type of bully that all the *bully spies* must find. At the same time, I will hold up the animal hat that matches the picture on the card. The *bully spies* will then call on different class members to see if anyone is that type of bully.**

If any of the *bully spies* calls on you and you are a *secret bully*, you must respond to the *bully spy,* speaking like the type of bully on the *Jungle Animal Card* chosen. If the *Jungle Animal Card* reads Croaking Crocodile, for example, and the *bully spy* calls on you, you need to yell at the *bully spy* because the Crocodile stands for *yelling*. If the card reads Walloping Warthog, and the *bully spy* calls on you, you need to give an answer that sounds like you are threatening the *bully spy*. Only *secret bullies* may respond this way. Please remember that we are role-playing. No one should try to intentionally hurt another person's feelings. Do not use the names of anyone in this school. Remember that no touching is allowed.

The *bully spies* will ask such questions as "Are you the bully?" or "What's for lunch?" or "What color do you like best?" These questions can be asked of more than one student. If you have not been tapped, answer the question respectfully, as you normally would. The *bully spies* will know, by the way you answer, whether you are a bully. After all six *bullies* have been identified, we will start a new game with another group of students.

Now put your heads down. I will secretly choose the six *bullies*.

Quickly go around the room and tap six students on the head. Then choose volunteers to be the *bully spies* and play the game.

Follow-Up:

At the conclusion of the activity, have the students answer the following:

How did the bully sound as the bully answered the *bully spy's* questions?

How would you feel if someone talking with you used one of the *Jungle Animal Card* traits?

PEEK-A-BOO BULLY

Purpose:

To help students recognize various types of bullies

Grade Levels: 2-5

Materials Needed:

For The Leader:

☐ *Jungle Animal Hats* (pages 197-255)
☐ Chalkboard and chalk (if you are using the song)

Pre-Lesson Preparation:

If not constructed previously, make each *Jungle Animal Hat* according to its directions.

Lesson:

Optional: Review some of the previously taught bully songs. If the songs are part of this presentation, write the following words on the chalkboard:

BULLY DON'T BOTHER ME

Bully don't bother me,
Bully don't bother me,
Bully don't bother me,
'Cause I am a SOMEBODY!

(*Note:* If the *Tyrannical Tiger—My Way Or No Way* lesson (page 67) has been presented, the students will have already learned *Bully Don't Bother Me*.)

Then tell the children:

Today we will learn/repeat the song *Bully Don't Bother Me* and we will sing it to the tune of *Shoo-Fly Don't Bother Me.* How many of you have heard or know that song? (Pause for responses.) **Can anyone sing one verse for us?** (Allow one or more students to sing a verse from *Shoo-Fly Don't Bother Me.*)

CONQUERING BULLIES © 2005 MAR✶CO PRODUCTS, INC. 1-800-448-2197

Help the students with any new words in *Bully Don't Bother Me.* Practice the words of the new song, line by line, with the class. Have the students repeat each line to you. Then have the students sing the song.

Game Procedure:

Place the *Jungle Animal Hats* where they can be seen by all of the students. Explain or review what type of bully each hat represents. Then introduce or continue the lesson by explaining the game procedure. Say:

> **Today we are going to pick out *bullies*. I will choose six people to come to the front of the room. They will cover their eyes with their hands as they did when they were very young and played *Peek-A-Boo*. When their eyes are covered, I will hold up one of the *Jungle Animal Hats* and point to one of you in the class to come to the front and wear the hat.**
>
> **The person wearing the hat will then say something that sounds like what the animal would say. For example, the student wearing the *Refusing Rhino* hat, could say, "I didn't write on the bathroom wall and you can't prove that I did. You probably did it yourself." This is because the *Refusing Rhino* always denies doing anything wrong. If necessary, I will help the person wearing the hat say something that sounds like the jungle animal.**
>
> **Please remember that we are role-playing. No one should try to intentionally hurt another person's feelings. Do not use the names of anyone in this school. No touching is allowed.**
>
> **Then I will ask each of the six people to tell what kind of bully he or she heard. After responding, each person may take his or her hands away and look to see if the answer was correct.**
>
> **Everyone who gives a correct answer may remain in the front of the room for another turn. However, after giving three correct answers, that person must retire. A new person will be chosen to take his or her place.**
>
> **A new person will wear a new animal hat for each round.**

Choose the first six students and begin the game.

Follow-Up:

At the conclusion of the activity, have the students answer the following:

> **Which bully was the most difficult to recognize?**
>
> **Which bully was the easiest to recognize?**

GUIDANCE LESSONS

DEALING WITH BULLIES

Nine games for grades 2-5 to give
students practice in confronting bullies

 # HIDE THE OSTRICH HEAD

Purpose:

To help students realize when someone denies bullying abuse

Grade Levels: 2-5

Materials Needed:

For The Leader:

☐ Copy of *Hot/Cold Statements* (page 158)
☐ Copy of *Ostrich Head Card* (page 159)
☐ Chalkboard and chalk (if you are using the song)
☐ Timer or clock with a second hand

Pre-Lesson Preparation:

Make a copy of the *Hot/Cold Statements* and the *Ostrich Head Card*. Laminate the *Ostrich Head Card* for durability.

Lesson:

Optional: Review some of the previously taught bully songs. If the songs are part of this presentation, write the following words on the chalkboard:

ALL AROUND THE PLAYGROUND

All around the playground he went.
The bully chased the children.
The bully thought it was all in fun,
"Stop!" said the children.

Then tell the children:

Today we will learn the song *All Around The Playground*, and we will sing it to the tune of *Pop Goes The Weasel*. How many of you have heard or know that song? (Pause for responses.) **Can anyone sing one verse for us?** (Allow one or more students to sing a verse from *Pop Goes The Weasel*.)

Help the students with any new words in *All Around The Playground.* Practice the words of the new song, line by line, with the class. Have the students repeat each line to you. Then have the students sing the song.

Introduce or continue the lesson by saying:

A person who sees or hears someone behaving like a bully sometimes tries to forget about what he or she has seen, ignore what happened, or deny that a person just acted like a bully. For example, someone acting the way a bully might act could say, "You're too dumb to play this game" or "Who would want to be your friend, anyway?" If a person pretends that it's okay for a bully to talk that way or denies that a person talking that way is a bully, that person is like the ostrich, an animal that hides its head in the sand if something bad is going on.

Game Procedure:

Continue the lesson by explaining the game procedure. Say:

Today we are going to practice finding the hidden *Ostrich Head Card*.

I will choose three children to hide their eyes. (Alternative: Have the three students step out of the room.) **I will then choose one person to hide the *Ostrich Head Card* somewhere in the room. The card should be hidden in a place that is not too easy to find, but is still visible.**

Then I will ask the three students to open their eyes (or step back into the room). **In order to find the hidden *Ostrich Head Card,* the three players must move together in the same direction around the room. As they move in one direction, the whole class will help guide them to the card by saying, "hot," "warm," or "cold." If the three players are far away from the hidden *Ostrich Head Card*, the class will say, "cold." If the three players are getting closer to the hidden *Ostrich Head Card*, the class will say, "warm." If the three players are very close to the hidden *Ostrich Head Card,* the class will say, "hot."**

But there is a catch! The three players cannot respond to the students' hint and change directions without first responding to a *Hot/Cold Statement*. After the class gives a "hot," "warm," or "cold" clue, I will read one statement aloud. The three players must then decide together whether the statement is "hot" or "cold." If the statement on the card is one that a bully might make, all three students must say, "cold." If the statement is one that a bully would not make, all three students in the group must say, "hot." The group of three may then continue moving in the new direction, whether the answer is correct or incorrect. If the answer is correct, the group will earn one point.

The group has only two minutes to find the hidden *Ostrich Head Card*. **If the card has not been found in two minutes, we will reveal its hiding place. I will record the group's points on the chalkboard and select a new group of three students to hide their eyes** (or step out of the room) **and a new person to hide the Ostrich Head Card. Then we will play another round of** *Hide The Ostrich Head.*

Choose three students to hide their eyes or leave the room. Choose a student to hide the *Ostrich Head Card*. Continue the game until the allotted time has elapsed.

Follow-Up:

At the conclusion of the activity, have the students answer the following:

What helped you decide if the statements you heard were "hot" or "cold"?

Is it helpful to hide, like the ostrich, from a bully? How can you do this?

 **SAFARI**

Purpose:

To help students understand the *Code of Silence* and learn when and why they should speak up against bullying and break this code

Grade Levels: 2-5

Materials Needed:

For The Leader:

☐ Copy of *Code Of Silence Cards* (pages 161-163)

For Each Student:

☐ *I've Been Working With A Bully* song (optional, page 160)

Pre-Lesson Preparation:

Make a copy of the *Code Of Silence Cards*. Cut apart the cards and laminate them for durability.

If you are using the songs, make a copy of *I've Been Working With A Bully* for each student.

Lesson:

Optional: Review some of the previously taught bully songs. Then give each student a copy of *I've Been Working With A Bully*. Say:

> **Today we will begin our lesson by learning a song about a bully. It is called *I've Been Working With A Bully*, and it is sung to the tune of *I've Been Working On The Railroad*. How many of you have heard or know that song?** (Pause for responses.) **Can anyone sing one verse for us?** (Allow one or more students to sing a verse of *I've Been Working On The Railroad*.)

Help the students with any new words in *I've Been Working With A Bully.* Practice the words of the new song, line by line, with the class. Have the students repeat each line to you. Then have the students sing the song.

Introduce or continue the lesson by saying:

> **Today we will learn how to break the *Code Of Silence* when dealing with a bully. What is a *safari*?** (Allow time for responses. Elicit answers such as *going hunting, finding jungle animals,* etc.) **We are going to pretend we are going on a safari today to hunt for sayings that people use to keep the *Code Of Silence* when they are being bullied or when they see someone else being bullied. It is important to recognize these sayings in order to break the *Code Of Silence* about bullying. Bullies depend upon this *Code Of Silence* in order not to have to face the consequences of their actions. If the person being bullied doesn't say anything because he or she is too afraid, is hoping that it doesn't happen again, or is ashamed about being picked on, then the *Code Of Silence* remains. So does the bully. If a person witnesses a bullying act and is too afraid to report what he or she has seen, the *Code Of Silence* remains unbroken. To put an end to bullying, we need to understand when to break the *Code Of Silence*.**

Game Procedure:

Continue the lesson by explaining the game procedure. Say:

> **I will choose three students to go on a *safari*. Then I will hand out a *Code Of Silence Card* to each of the other students in the class. The three students going on the *safari* will take turns calling on someone in the class to read his or her *Code Of Silence Card* aloud. The card might say, "I will help you." By saying this, you would be breaking the *Code Of Silence* and helping a classmate who is being bullied. But a *Code Of Silence Card* might also say, "There is nothing I can do." By not helping the person being bullied, you are encouraging the bully, and the *Code Of Silence* remains unbroken. If a student reads a statement that *Breaks The Code Of Silence*, the card is given to the player who chose him or her to read.**

> **The three chosen players need to capture three cards that *Break The Code Of Silence*. The winner in the group is the first person to collect three cards that *Break The Code Of Silence*.**

> **Let's begin our safari.**

Select three students to go on the *safari*. Distribute the *Code Of Silence Cards* and begin the game.

Follow-Up:

At the conclusion of the activity, have the students answer the following:

Were you surprised by the statements that *do not* break the *Code Of Silence?* Why or why not?

How would you feel if the *Code Of Silence* was not broken?

LITTLE RASCALS

(*Note:* This lesson should not be presented until you have taught several of the other lessons in this program.)

Purpose:

To help students learn how to get the support of friends in a bad situation

Grade Levels: 2-5

Materials Needed:

For The Leader:

☐ *Jungle Animal Hats* from previously taught lessons
☐ Four or five handkerchief-size pieces of material
☐ Copy of *Little Rascals Situation Cards* (pages 164-165)
☐ Copy of *Little Rascals Bully Cards* (page 165)
☐ Chalkboard and chalk (if you are using the song)

Pre-Lesson Preparation:

Make a copy of the *Little Rascals Situation Cards* and the *Little Rascals Bully Cards*. Cut apart the cards and laminate them for durability.

Lesson:

Optional: Review some of the previously taught bully songs. If the songs are part of this presentation, write the following words on the chalkboard:

TEN LITTLE FRIENDS

One little, two little, three little friends,
Four little, five little, six little friends,
Seven little, eight little, nine little friends,
Ten little friends against bullies.

Ten little, nine little, eight little friends,
Seven little, six little, five little friends,
four little, three little, two little friends,
One little friend against bullies.

Then tell the children:

> **Today we will learn the song _Ten Little Friends_. We will sing it to the tune of _Ten Little Indians_. How many of you have heard or know that song?** (Pause for responses.) **Can anyone sing one verse for us?** (Allow one or more students to sing a verse of _Ten Little Indians_.)

Help the students with any new words in _Ten Little Friends._ Practice the words of the new song, line by line, with the class. Have the students repeat each line to you. Then have the students sing the song.

Place the _Jungle Animal Hats_ where they can be seen by the entire class. Then introduce or continue the lesson by saying:

> **Today we are going to review and practice what we have learned about supporting friends who are dealing with bullies. We know that having the support of your friends in a bad situation can help you in many ways. Can you name some ways supporting friends can help the person who is being bullied?** (Allow time for responses. Elicit answers such as: _It shows the bully that teamwork and sticking up for the wronged person can help that person feel better about him/herself. It shows the bully that everyone knows what is happening. It provides a good role model for the bully to begin changing his/her ways. It shows the bully that people are not going to stand by and accept bullying behavior,_ etc.)

> **How many of you have watched _The Little Rascals_ on TV or DVD? What are some ways they stick together?** (Allow time for responses. Elicit answers such as: _By sticking together they helped each other when one of them was in trouble, did not give up in a bad situation, did not leave someone out,_ etc.)

> **We have learned that by sticking together, friends support one another and _can_ stand up against bullies. Today we're going to practice being the _Little Rascals Group._**

Game Procedure:

Continue the lesson by explaining the game procedure. Say:

> **I will divide the class into four or five small groups.** (If there is an unequal number of students, adjust the number in each group to make the groups as even as possible. Have at least four students in each group, but no more than seven. You may form the groups by having the students count off from 1 to 4 or 5, by grouping rows together, etc.) **I will give each group one _Situation Card_. The groups will have three minutes to work together to organize a skit, based on the _Situation Card,_ that demonstrates how friends can support one another when confronted by a bully. In each skit, one person will portray the _bully_. No one will know who the _bully_ is until each group member has picked a _Bully Card_.**

When it is your group's turn to present your skit, your group will come to the front of the class. At that time, each of you will place a handkerchief in your pants pocket or waistband. Tuck in only the corner of the handkerchief, leaving most of it hanging loose. (If any student does not have a waistband or pants pocket, suggest another place to put the handkerchief.) **Then each group member will draw one *Bully Card*.** (*Note:* If there are fewer than seven group members, reduce the number of cards to match the number of students in the group. Be sure one of the remaining cards is the *Bully Card*.) **Only one of the cards will have the word *Bully* printed on it. The group members *must* keep what is written on their cards secret from one another.**

As the skit is being presented, the person with the *Bully Card* must role-play any of the types of bullying behavior we have practiced in other lessons. As soon as any of the group members recognizes the type of bullying being demonstrated, that person should take the handkerchief from the *bully's* pocket or waistband. The person removing the handkerchief must grab the handkerchief without touching the *bully*. The first group member to do so helps the team win applause from our class for sticking up for the others and for being able to recognize the *bully*. The person grabbing the handkerchief will then select the *Jungle Animal Hat* that relates to the bullying trait the group member portrayed and place it on the *bully's* head. The rest of group members will then name what clues helped them to find the *bully* in their group.

Divide the students into groups. Place the *Little Rascals Bully Cards* on a table near the front of the room. Distribute one *Little Rascals Situation Card* to each group. Begin timing the groups for three minutes. When three minutes has elapsed, select one group to come to the front of the room. Have each group member choose a *Bully Card*, then role-play its skit. Continue this procedure until all of the groups have presented their skits.

Follow-Up:

At the conclusion of the activity, have the students who portrayed bullies in the skits answer the following:

How did you feel when the other group members stuck together to stop the *bully*?

How did you feel about being the person with the *Bully Card?*

Then have the students answer the following:

How do you think a "real" bully would feel if everyone stuck together against him or her?

 # CONFRONTING THE BEAST

Purpose:

To teach students when it is safe to confront a bully and to respond in a positive, safe way to a bully

Grade Levels: 2-5

Materials Needed:

For The Leader:

☐ *Jungle Animal Hats* (4 hats for grades K-1, 8 hats for grades 2-3, and all 12 hats for grades 4-6, pages 197-255)
☐ Copy of *Jungle Animal Cards* (pages 149-150)
☐ Chalkboard and chalk (if you are using the song)

Pre-Lesson Preparation:

Select the *Jungle Animal Hats* to be used in the lesson and the correlating *Jungle Animal Cards.* If not constructed previously, make each hat according to its directions.

Make a copy of the *Jungle Animal Cards.* Cut apart the cards and laminate them for durability.

Lesson:

Optional: Review some of the previously taught bully songs. If the songs are part of this presentation, write the following words on the chalkboard:

THE PIGITY, WIGITY BULLY

The pigity, wigity bully
Climbed up the jungle gym.
Out came the shouts:
"Stay away from him."
Down came the bully
And away the bully ran.
Then up went the class
To play because they can.

Then tell the children:

Today we will learn the song *The Pigity, Wigity Bully*. We will sing it to the tune of *The Itsy, Bitsy Spider*. How many of you have heard or know that song? (Pause for responses.) **Can anyone sing one verse for us?** (Allow one or more students to sing a verse of *The Pigity, Wigity Bully*.)

Help the students with any new words in *The Pigity, Wigity Bully*. Practice the words of the new song, line by line, with the class. Have the students repeat each line to you. Then have the students sing the song.

Place the *Jungle Animal Hats* where they can be seen by the entire class. Then introduce or continue the lesson by saying:

Today we are going to learn the most positive and safe ways to confront a *bully beast*. *Confronting* means acknowledging the bully or letting the bully know that you realize he or she is a bully. Always be safe when you confront a bully. You need to have a friend or an adult with you when you confront a bully.

Let's think of some positive things you can say or do to when confronting a bully.

If not mentioned by the students, suggest some of the following things they could say to a bully:

That makes no sense.
That is not right.
Let's check that out with the teacher.
We need to discuss that with the teacher.
I wonder what my dad will say about that.
I heard that line on TV.
Maybe they sell that stuff at some stores, but not here.
So what!
Keep it clean.
Take out the trash talk.

Game Procedure:

Continue the lesson by explaining the game procedure. Say:

I will choose several students to each wear a different *Jungle Animal Hat*. (Choose between 4 and 12 students. Select fewer students for younger, less advanced groups.) **These students will pretend to be *bully beasts*. Each of the students wearing a hat will also be given a matching *Jungle Animal Card*. Printed on the card will**

be a picture of that student's *Jungle Animal Hat*. The students chosen will read what is printed on their *Jungle Animal Cards*. When you read your card, use lots of expression to demonstrate the type of bully you represent.

I will choose two students from the class to come up to any three *bully beasts* and say, "Hi." The bullies will answer by saying one of the statements written on the *Jungle Animal Card*.

The person saying "Hi" has five seconds to confront the bully by responding with a positive, safe statement that he or she feels comfortable making. Because it is best to have a friend who can help you out in a bad situation, the *friend* can also help by responding to the bully.

If the two *friends* successfully make a positive, safe response, the *bully* must give his or her hat to them. The *friends* can then approach the next bully. If the two *friends* make a negative or unsafe response, they must return to their seats, and I will select two new *friends* to come the front of the class. If the pair collects three hats, they may choose the next pair of *friends* to *Confront The Beast*. They may also choose three new people from the class to wear the collected hats and select matching *Jungle Animal Cards*. The *friends* can choose themselves to wear the hats and play *bully beasts* in the next round.

Select the students who will be wearing the hats. Give each of them the appropriate *Jungle Animal Card.* Choose two *friends* and begin the game. Continue the game for as long as time allows.

Follow-Up:

At the conclusion of the activity, have the students answer the following:

To which type of *bully beast* was it the most difficult to respond?

To which type of *bully beast* was it the easiest to respond?

CONQUERING BULLIES © 2005 MAR*CO PRODUCTS, INC. 1-800-448-2197

 **POT SHOT**

Purpose:

To give children an opportunity to practice using positive comebacks to use when dealing with a bully

Grade Levels: 2-5

Materials Needed:

For The Leader:

☐ Copy of *Pot Shot Statements And Situations* (page 167)
☐ Chalkboard and chalk

For Each Student:

☐ Copy of *If You Need To Answer A Bully* song (optional, page 166)

Pre-Lesson Preparation:

Make a copy of *Pot Shot Statements And Situations.*

If you are using the songs, make a copy of *If You Need To Answer A Bully* for each student.

Lesson:

Optional: Review some of the previously taught bully songs. Then give each student a copy of *If You Need To Answer A Bully.* Say:

> **Today we will begin our lesson by learning a song about what to do when we have to answer a bully. The way we answer a bully can make the situation worse or actually make it better. This song suggests ways to answer a bully that can make the situation you are in better. These ideas or answers are called *positive comebacks.* The word *positive* means *helpful* or *certain.* A *comeback* is *a response to an answer. If You Need To Answer A Bully* is sung to the tune of *If You're Happy And You Know It.* How many of you have heard or know that song?**

(Pause for responses.) **Can anyone sing one verse for us?** (Allow one or more students to sing a verse of *If You're Happy And You Know It.*)

As you review the *positive comebacks* in the song (bold-faced type on lyric sheet), write each one on the board: Make a deal, Look surprised, Yell out "STOP!", Compliment, Agree, Ignore, and Make a Joke. Practice the words of the new song, line by line, with the class. Have the students repeat each line to you. Then have the students sing the song.

Introduce or continue the lesson by saying:

> **In today's lesson, we will learn some positive comebacks you can use when dealing with a bully. These comebacks should not be used to antagonize or anger the bully. They are meant to ease a bad situation and help you not feel defenseless. By practicing comebacks, you will be more prepared to respond to a bully if the situation arises. Later in the lesson, we will be voting on which comebacks you feel would work best.**

Game Procedure:

Continue the lesson by explaining the game procedure. Say:

> **The game we are going to play is called *Pot Shot*. In this game, I will choose two of the positive comebacks you have suggested for use in a bullying situation. After hearing both positive comebacks, you will choose the one you would be most comfortable using. There are no right or wrong answers. Just select the positive comeback you believe you would be able to use and still feel good about yourself.**
>
> **I will read a type of bullying situation or a comment a bully might make. Raise your hand if you can think of a positive comeback you would make in this situation. Remember: Your response should be positive. Do not use put-downs, name-calling, yelling, or say anything that a bully might say. From your answers, I will choose two clever comebacks. The students whose comebacks I choose will stand and walk to opposite sides of the room. Then I will call for students at each table (or in each row) to walk over and stand by the person who made the comeback they feel they would be most comfortable using.**
>
> **Although we will see which positive comeback is the favorite, we need to remember that the other comeback can be just as effective. There are no right or wrong choices. Before we begin, remember the ideas on the board.** (Point to the board and review the ideas if necessary.)
>
> **Let's begin.**

Using the *Pot Shot Statements And Situations,* begin the game. Continue the game for as long as time allows.

Follow-Up:

At the conclusion of the activity, have the students answer the following:

Which positive statement was the best one for you to use?

Tell which situations mentioned you have been in and what you did. Do not mention any names.

If you were in that same situation now, what would you do?

 # THROUGH THE JUNGLE

Purpose:

To teach students to practice quick thinking when confronted by a bully

Grade Levels: 3-5

Materials Needed:

For The Leader:

☐ Number of *Jungle Animal Hats* equal to the number of players in the game (pages 197-255)
☐ Chalkboard and chalk

For Each Student:

☐ Copy of *Answering The Bully* song (optional, page 168)

Pre-Lesson Preparation:

Select the *Jungle Animal Hats* to be used in the lesson. If not constructed previously, make each hat according to its directions.

If you are using the songs, make a copy of *Answering The Bully* for each student.

Lesson:

Optional: Review some of the previously taught bully songs. Then give each student a copy of *Answering The Bully*.

Then say:

> **Today we will begin our lesson by learning the song *Answering The Bully*. This song is about answering a bully with a positive comeback. The song is sung to the tune of *Skip To My Lou*. How many of you have heard or know that song?** (Pause for responses.) **Can anyone sing one verse for us?** (Allow one or more students to sing a verse of *Skip To My Lou*.)

Review the key words in the song (in bold on the lyric sheet), and write them on the chalk-board. *(Make a joke for the bully. I agree with the bully. Apologize to the bully. You sure surprised me, Bully.)* Underline the words *joke, agree, apologize,* and *surprised.* Then say:

These are the positive comebacks that we are going to learn about today. Now let's sing our song.

Introduce or continue the lesson by saying:

Today we are going to practice responding to a bully with a positive comeback by making a joke, agreeing, apologizing, and acting surprised. In order to do this, you need to remember:

> **Making a joke is saying something funny about what the bully is saying. If the bully is saying you are not good at sports, for example, you might answer, "Do you think dropping the ball 1,000 times during the last game means I'm not a good player?"**

> **Agreeing with the bully should be done only if you believe the bully could be right. If the bully is making fun of you because you wear glasses, for example, you might answer, "I know, but having four eyes makes me see twice as well as anyone with two eyes."**

> **Apologizing is really not making a sincere apology. It is just an answer that says you are sorry for having or doing what the bully is saying. If the bully is making fun of your physical appearance, for example, you might say, "I'm sorry I have red hair, but it's a family trait."**

> **Acting surprised shows the bully that you can hardly believe what you have heard. If the bully says you are the poorest reader in the class, for example, you might respond, "What? Where did you get that information? I can't believe you said that!"**

Game Procedure:

Continue the lesson by introducing the game:

Today we are going to walk through the jungle on an animal path. This is the path where the bullies of the jungle can be found, and you need to be ready in case you meet up with one of them. You must be prepared with different comebacks for these bullies in order to get to the end of the path.

Who would like to volunteer to be one of the *bullies*? If you are a *bully*, you will need to say something that the animal you are portraying would say. If you are the Tyrannical Tiger, for example, you must act bossy. Please remember this is only role-playing. No one should try to intentionally hurt another person's feelings. No touching is allowed.

I need (<u>NUMBER OF BULLIES FROM 4-12 THAT YOU WANT THE STUDENTS TO ENCOUNTER</u>) volunteers. Raise your hand if you would like to be a volunteer.

Select the volunteers. Give each volunteer a *Jungle Animal Hat.* Tell the students what bullying behavior each of the hats stand for.

Loud-Mouth Lion is a gossip.
Hurtful Hyena leaves others out of groups.
Walloping Warthog is threatening.
Tyrannical Tiger is bossy.
Zany Zebra always denies doing anything wrong.
Erupting Elephant puts others down.
Gloating Giraffe acts snooty.
Menacing Monkey frightens people.
Harassing Hippo calls others names.
Refusing Rhino lies.
Snappy Snake acts rude.

Have the *bullies* stand in a straight line along the side of the room. Then say:

Now I need two volunteers to walk together down the jungle path and help each other think of positive comebacks. You will have only 10 seconds to say a different positive comeback to each *bully* who has said something to you. You must try hard to get to the end of the jungle path. If you don't beat the 10-second time limit each time you meet up with a *bully*, you must leave the path and two new travelers will be chosen. At that time, the *bullies* will change places along the path so each set of volunteers will not face the *bullies* in the same order as the last volunteers. The timing will start immediately after the *bully* has made his or her statement to you.

Let's review who the *bullies* are and what they might say. As I call each of your names, the student role-playing this *bully* should take a step forward from the line, then step back into line. Loud-Mouth Lion is a gossip, Hurtful Hyena leaves others out of groups, Walloping Warthog is threatening, Tyrannical Tiger is bossy, Zany Zebra always denies doing anything wrong, Erupting Elephant puts others down, Gloating Giraffe acts snooty, Menacing Monkey frightens people, Harassing Hippo calls others names, Refusing Rhino lies, and Snappy Snake acts rude.

Have the first two volunteers begin walking down the path, timing their response as each *bully* confronts them. When their turn is over, have the *bullies* change places on the path. Then continue with two new volunteers. Continue the game until everyone has had a turn or the allotted time has elapsed.

Follow-Up:

At the conclusion of the activity, have the students answer the following:

Which bully statement was the most difficult to respond to with a positive comeback?

Which bully statement was the easiest to give a positive comeback?

 # JUNGLE SURVIVOR

Purpose:

To help students learn to survive in a comeback standoff

Grade Levels: 3-5

Materials Needed:

For The Leader:

☐ *Erupting Elephant Cards* (optional, pages 173-174)
☐ *Jungle Animal Cards* (optional, pages 149-150)
☐ Different colors of construction paper
☐ Scissors
☐ Chalkboard and chalk or dry-erase board and marker

Pre-Lesson Preparation:

Obtain descriptions of bullying situations from the *Erupting Elephant Cards*, *Jungle Animal Cards*, or make up four or five situations that would be relevant to the group.

Cut the construction paper into strips.

Optional: Prior to presenting the lesson, write the positive comebacks and ways they could be used (see page 48) on the board.

Lesson:

Introduce the lesson by saying:

> **In today's lesson, we will be reviewing/learning to make positive comebacks. These are ways to respond that may not anger the bully and make the situation worse. Of course, there are no guarantees. But using positive comebacks is the best chance anyone has of dealing effectively with a bully.**

On the board, write the following positive comebacks and ways they could be used. As each technique is written, read it aloud.

- Agree with the bully if you feel what the bully said could be true.
  Say, "You are right. I'm not good at softball."

- Make a joke out of what was said.
  Say, "I probably couldn't catch a softball if I had *two* mitts."

- Distract the bully by asking him/her an unrelated question.
  Ask, "What time is lunch?"

- Give the bully a compliment.
  Say, "I like your shirt."

- Make a deal with the bully.
  Say, "If you stop that, I'll help you with math."

- Use old sayings.
  Say, "Sticks and stones may break my bones, but names will never hurt me."

- Act surprised or shocked.
  Say, "I'm surprised you said that."

- Apologize to the bully by saying something that is related to the bully's comment.
  Say, "I'm sorry I have blonde hair."

- Ignore the bully.
  Say nothing. Give the bully no verbal or physical recognition.

- Be assertive.
  Say, "Stop that right now."

Before continuing, ask the students:

Are there any other positive comebacks that you would like to add to our list?
(Pause for student responses. Add any possibilities not already listed on the board.)

Game Procedure:

Introduce the game by saying:

> **We are going to practice surviving in the *Bully Jungle.* In order to do this, you will be divided into small teams of three or four members. Each team will be assigned a number, and each person on the team will take a turn calling out a positive comeback. I will begin the game by choosing two teams to play the first round. I will read a description of a bullying situation. The first person to call out an appropriate positive comeback earns a colored strip for his or her team. The team with the most colored strips at the end of the game will be declared the winner. Your team members can help you by whispering a response or comeback to you. If neither team makes a response within one minute, I will call on two other teams to continue the game. If you need a clue, look at the possibilities listed on the board. A team member who has called out a comeback may not call out again until each of the other members of the team has also called out a comeback. This will give everyone a chance to practice positive comebacks.**

Divide the students into small teams of three or four members. Assign each team a number. Then say:

> **Remember, I will call out two team numbers for each round. For example, I might say: "Team One and Team Six." The first team member to make a positive comeback related to the bullying situation I describe will earn a colored strip for his or her team.**

Begin the game. Give each team the same number of turns.

Follow-Up:

At the conclusion of the activity, have the students answer the following:

> **What helped you think of a positive comeback?**

> **How did your team help you?**

> **How are friends important in dealing with a bully?**

 # PHOTO OPPORTUNITY

(*Note:* This lesson should not be presented until the students are familiar with each of the types of bullies and have learned appropriate comeback techniques.)

Purpose:

To help students learn to respond to a bullying situation with appropriate positive comebacks

Grade Levels: 4-5

Materials Needed:

For The Leader:

☐ *Erupting Elephant Cards* (optional, pages 173-174)
☐ *Jungle Animal Cards* (optional, pages 149-150)
☐ Chalkboard and chalk or dry-erase board and marker

Pre-Lesson Preparation:

Obtain descriptions of bullying situations from the *Erupting Elephant Cards*, *Jungle Animal Cards*, or make up four or five situations that would be relevant to the group.

Optional: Prior to presenting the lesson, write the positive comebacks and suggestions for illustrations (see page 51) on the board.

Lesson:

Introduce the lesson by saying:

> **In order to deal with bullies, it is important to know what to do in different bullying situations. How many of you like to draw pictures?** (Pause for student responses.) **In today's lesson, you will be drawing pictures that show positive responses to bullying instead of *saying* them aloud.**
>
> **Let's review some responses to bullying and ways you could illustrate them.**

On the board, write the following positive comebacks and suggestions for illustrations. As you write each technique and suggestion, read it aloud.

- Agree with the bully if you feel what the bully said is true.
  You might draw a picture of a person nodding his or her head to indicate "yes."

- Make a joke of what was said.
  You might draw a picture of a person laughing.

- Distract the bully.
  You might draw a picture of a person showing the bully a new video game.

- Give the bully a compliment.
  You might draw a picture of someone patting the bully on the back.

- Make a deal with the bully.
  You might draw a picture of two people giving each other high-fives.

- Use old sayings.
  You might draw a picture to illustrate "Sticks and stones may break my bones, but names will never hurt me" by showing sticks breaking bones.

- Act surprised or shocked.
  You might draw a picture of someone looking surprised.

- Apologize to the bully.
  You might draw a picture of a person looking sorry.

- Ignore the bully.
  You might draw a picture of someone walking away from the bully.

- Be assertive.
  You might draw a picture of someone looking directly into the bully's face.

Game Procedure:

Divide the class into four or five teams. Instruct the teams to sit to together. Then say:

I will assign a number to each team member. This number will determine the order in which each team member will to go to the board. Don't forget your number. When everyone has a number, I will ask the first member of each team— Team Member #1—to come to the board.

I will describe a bullying situation. The team members will have one minute to draw a positive comeback to the situation on the board. The person who is drawing may not use any words, only picture clues. You may choose the same positive comeback technique as someone else, but your drawing must be of something that has not been drawn before. If a person chooses to draw a picture of a child making a joke, for example, and draws a picture of a child laughing, another person could not draw a picture of someone laughing. The picture would have to be different. This means you will have to remember what has already been drawn not only by your team members, but also by members of other teams. When I tell you to begin, the team members at the board will have one minute to complete their drawings.

When I call "*Time*," each team will have three chances to describe which positive comeback technique its team member drew. If the team members guess on the first try, the team will be awarded three points. If they guess on the second try, the team will be awarded two points. If they guess on the third try, the team will be awarded one point. Team members must raise their hands to guess. The student who made the drawing will call on a team member whose hand is raised.

Begin the game. Continue playing until every team member has drawn a picture or the allotted time has elapsed.

Follow-Up:

At the conclusion of the activity, have the students answer the following:

Which positive comeback was easiest to draw?

Which positive comeback was most difficult to draw?

Is it easier to *draw* a positive comeback or to *say* a positive comeback? Why?

 **JEEP TRAIL RIDERS**

(*Note:* This lesson should not be presented until the students are familiar with each of the types of bullies and have learned appropriate comeback techniques.)

Purpose:

To help students learn to respond to a bullying situation with an appropriate positive comeback

Grade Levels: 3-5

Materials Needed:

For The Leader:

☐ *Jungle Animal Hats* (number determined by the age of the students and the number of types of bullies the leader wishes to include)
☐ Chalkboard and chalk or dry-erase board and marker

For Each Student:

☐ Numbered index card

Pre-Lesson Preparation:

Write a number from 1 to 5 on each index card. Be sure to have enough cards for each student to receive one. You may want to make several extra cards, repeating the numbers from 1 to 5 or using zeros.

Optional: Prior to presenting the lesson, write the positive comebacks and possible ways they can be used (see page 54) on the board.

Lesson:

Introduce the lesson by saying:

We have learned about the different types of bullies and how to use positive comebacks to respond to bullying situations. Today we are going to play a game using (<u>NUMBER OF TYPES OF BULLIES CHOSEN</u>) different types of bullies. You will be asked to respond to each of these bullies with a positive comeback.

Let's review the positive comebacks you can use.

On the board, write the following positive comebacks and possible ways they can be used. As you write each technique, read it aloud.

- Agree with the bully if you feel what the bully said is true.
  Say, "You are right. I'm not good at _____ ."

- Make a joke of what was said.
  Say, "Even 10,000 tutors couldn't help me get a good grade in math."

- Distract the bully by asking him or her an unrelated question.
  Ask, "What video game did you say you like best?"

- Give the bully a compliment.
  Say, "I like your shirt."

- Make a deal with the bully.
  Say, "If you stop (<u>IDENTIFY THE BULLY'S BEHAVIOR</u>), I'll help you get better grades."

- Use old sayings.
  Say, "Sticks and stones may break my bones, but names will never hurt me."

- Act surprised or shocked.
  Say, "I can't believe you really said that!"

- Apologize to the bully.
  Say, "I'm sorry that (<u>IDENTIFY WHAT THE BULLY IS TARGETING ABOUT YOU</u>)."

- Ignore the bully.
  Give the bully no attention. Say nothing. Do nothing.

- Be assertive.
  Say, "Stop acting like a bully."

Game Procedure:

Introduce the game by saying:

> In today's game, we are going practice making positive comebacks. In order to do this, you will be divided into teams of three or four members. I will choose one team to come to the front of the room and go on the Jeep Trail. These Jeep Trail *riders* can choose anyone in the class to portray the bullies. The students selected will come to the front of the room, decide what type of bully they want to portray, and choose the *Jungle Animal Hat* that represents that type of bully. The *bullies* will wear the hats as we play each round of the game.
>
> I will give each *bully* an index card with a number printed on it. Each bully should stand near the front of the room. The Jeep Trail *riders* will then "drive" from *bully* to *bully*. When the *riders* reach a *bully*, the *bully* will make a statement that reflects the type of bully he or she is portraying. The Jeep Trail *riders* should respond with an appropriate positive comeback. If the *riders* respond appropriately, they will earn the number of points on the *bully's* card. I will collect the *bully's* card and keep it as a record of the team's win. The *riders* will continue to "drive" from *bully* to *bully* until they have responded to whatever each *bully* has said. That will be the end of the first round of the game. I will choose a new team to come to the front of the room. The new team will choose new *bullies* and we will play another round.
>
> Please remember this is only role-playing. No one should try to intentionally hurt another person's feelings. No touching is allowed.

Divide the students into teams. Have the first team come to the front of the room and choose *bullies*. (*Note:* The number of *bullies* chosen should equal the number of hats you are using in the lesson.) Tell the *bullies* to select a hat, then give each *bully* an index card. Begin the game. Continue playing until the allotted time has elapsed.

Follow-Up:

At the conclusion of the activity, have the students answer the following:

> How did you feel when you were responding to a bully?
>
> Without using names, tell if a bully has ever made a similar statement to you. What happened?
>
> Which positive comeback is the most useful for you?
>
> Which positive comeback do you think you would probably *not* use?

CONQUERING BULLIES © 2005 MAR✶CO PRODUCTS, INC. 1-800-448-2197

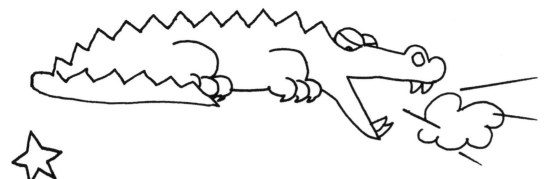

GUIDANCE LESSONS

TYPES OF BULLIES

Twelve activity-oriented lessons for grades 2-5
to give students information on different
bullying characteristics and strategies for dealing with them

LOUD-MOUTH LION
GOSSIPING

Purpose:

To help students become aware that something that is repeated may differ from what was said originally

Grade Levels: 2-5

Materials Needed:

For The Leader:

☐ *Loud-Mouth Lion Hat* (pages 198-202)
☐ Copy of *Loud-Mouth Lion Gossiping Statements* (page 169)
☐ Chalkboard and chalk (if you are using the song)

Pre-Lesson Preparation:

If not constructed previously, make the *Loud-Mouth Lion Hat* according to its directions.

Make a copy of the *Loud-Mouth Lion Gossiping Statements*.

Lesson:

Optional: Pick one or two of the previously taught bully songs to review. If the songs are part of this presentation, write the following words on the chalkboard:

WHERE IS GOSSIP?

Where is gossip?
Where is gossip?
Here it is. (point to mouth)
Here it is. (point to mouth)
Think before you talk. (point to head)
Think before you talk. (point to head)
Never gossip.
Never gossip.

Then tell the children:

Today we will learn the song *Where Is Gossip?* **We will sing it to the tune of** *Where Is Thumbkin?* **How many of you have heard or know that song?** (Pause for responses.) **Can anyone sing one verse for us?** (Allow one or more students to sing a verse of *Where Is Thumbkin?*)

Help the students with any new words in *Where Is Gossip?* Practice the words of the new song, line by line, with the class. Have the students repeat each line to you. Then have the students sing the song.

Introduce or continue the lesson by saying:

When someone makes a statement about another person that is hurtful and/or not necessarily true, it is called *gossip.* **Today we will learn how something told to you about another person might be repeated incorrectly. Spreading a rumor might upset the other person and the information might not be true. Gossiping is hurtful.**

Our jungle animal to represent gossip is the lion. (Hold up the *Loud-Mouth Lion Hat.*) **The lion's roar is so loud, it can be heard for miles. When a lion roars, other animals fear that the lion might come close, attack, and hurt them. A bully who gossips behaves the same way as a lion, using his or her loud mouth to attack and hurt someone. What kinds of statements would be gossip?** (Pause for responses. Possible answers could include talking in a negative way about how someone looks or spreading rumors about something the person might have done or said.) **When we compliment someone, we are being kind. When we gossip, we may hurt or upset someone.**

Game Procedure:

Continue the lesson by explaining the game procedure. Say:

I will divide you into groups of (select a number from 8-10) **members. I want each group to line up in rows** (or sit together at a table). **Each group will take a turn while the other groups watch and observe. Decide which of your group members will go first, second, third, and so forth. Line up (sit) in that order. I will whisper a statement to the first person in your group. Then that person will whisper to the next person. Then each person in the** *gossiping group* **will continue whispering what he or she has heard to the next person until the last person hears what was said. The last person in line will then announce what he or she heard. Remember: You may only whisper to the next person once, so make what you say as clear as you can. We'll see if what the last person heard matches what I said to the first person.**

The groups who are watching will report what they observed after the *gossiping group* has finished.

Divide the students into groups. Select one group to begin the activity. Using the *Loud-Mouth Lion Gossiping Statements,* whisper a statement into the first person's ear. After the last person in the group tells the class what he/she heard, discuss how this activity relates to gossiping. Continue the game until each group has had a turn.

Follow-Up:

At the conclusion of the activity, have the students respond to the following:

What do you think of gossiping now that you have seen it in action?

What can you do to stop any gossiping?

HURTFUL HYENA
LEAVING OTHERS OUT

Purpose:

To teach students how to recognize a bully who tries to exclude others

Grade Levels: 2-5

Materials Needed:

For The Leader:

☐ *Hurtful Hyena Hat* (pages 203-207)
☐ Copy of *Response Cards* (pages 170-171)
☐ Chalkboard and chalk

Pre-Lesson Preparation:

If not constructed previously, make the *Hurtful Hyena Hat* according to its directions.

Make two sets of the *Response Cards*. Cut the cards apart and laminate them for durability.

Optional: Prior to presenting the lesson, write the four steps in handling bullies (see page 62) on the chalkboard.

Lesson:

Optional: Pick one or two of the previously taught bully songs to review. If the songs are part of this presentation, write the following words on the chalkboard:

HURTFUL HYENA

Hurtful Hyena sadly leaves you out.
Find a friend, find a friend,
And clear up all your doubt.

Then tell the children:

Today we will learn the song *Hurtful Hyena*. We will sing it to the tune of *Row, Row, Row Your Boat*. How many of you have heard or know that song? (Pause for responses.) **Can anyone sing one verse for us?** (Allow one or more students to sing a verse of *Row, Row, Row Your Boat*.)

Help the students with any new words in *Hurtful Hyena*. Practice the words of the new song, line by line, with the class. Have the students repeat each line to you. Then have the students sing the song.

Introduce or continue the lesson by saying:

Today we are going to practice recognizing a bully who tries to exclude others or leave them out of a group. The hyena is a good jungle animal to use for this activity. (Hold up the *Hurtful Hyena Hat*.) **The hyena has a lot of power and gathers his clan or group together so other hyenas can't join that group. In fact, if they try to become part of that hyena's group, great battles take place.**

Ask the students the following questions:

How would you feel if someone tried to leave you out of a group? (Your feelings could be hurt; you could feel angry, helpless, or all alone; or any other appropriate answer.)

What might someone say to you when he or she tries to leave you out? (He/she might say, "Go away! We don't want you to play with us," "You don't know how to play this game," "You're too little," "We're saving that seat for someone else," or any other appropriate answer.)

Introduce or review the four steps in handling bullies. Write the following four steps on the chalkboard:

1. Be alert! Recognize a bully's actions or words.

2. Confront the bully. Tell the bully what he/she said or did.

3. Confirm what the bully is doing or talk with others about it. What can you say to others who are witnesses?

4. Support and help others. Be there for others if they are being bullied.

Then say:

These are the four ways you can respond to a bully who is leaving you or someone else out.

Continue the lesson by saying aloud or writing on the chalkboard examples of what could be said to a bully who is leaving someone out. Discuss the examples after writing each strategy.

1. Be alert! Recognize a bully's actions or words. Ask, "What did you say?"

2. Confront the bully. Tell the bully what he/she said or did. Say, "You sound like you're trying to leave _____ out. If that's what you're doing, then you're acting like a bully."

62

3. Confirm what the bully is doing or talk with others about it. What can you say to others who are witnesses? Ask, "Do you think he/she is leaving _____ out of the group?"

4. Support and help others. Be there for others if they are being bullied. Say, "Don't treat him/her that way."

Game Procedure:

Continue the lesson by explaining the game procedure. Say:

> **Let's begin the *Hurtful Hyena Game.* I will give a *Response Card* to everyone in the class, except one person. The person who does not get a *Response Card* will be *It.* The person playing *It* will wear the *Hurtful Hyena Hat. It* will call on two classmates to read their *Response Cards.* If their *Response Cards* match, the students will try to trade seats. The person who is *It* must try to sit in one of those students' seats before they complete the trade. If *It* successfully beats one of the students to a seat, the person left standing becomes the new *It.* If *It* does not beat either of the students to a seat, he or she remains *It.* Remember: No pushing or running.**

> **If the students' *Response Cards* don't match, *It* will choose two other class-mates to read their cards aloud. *It* will continue to choose people this way until there is a match. *It* should try to remember what was read from each *Response Card.* By memorizing what was said, *It* can move closer to the seat of one of the students whose *Response Card* might be a match. Then when *It* calls on two people who begin to change seats, *It* can get one of the seats first.**

> ***It* is like a bully who tries to leave someone out. So unless you are the person who starts the game, you should try your best not to be *It.* Are there any questions?**

Select a volunteer to be *It.* Give him/her the *Hurtful Hyena* hat to wear. Have the rest of the students form a circle with their chairs. Instruct *It* to stand in the center of the circle. (If it is not possible for the children to place their chairs in a circle, have them remain at their desks and instruct *It* to stand in the front of the room.) Distribute a *Response Card* to each student who is not *It.* Continue the game until the allotted time has elapsed or every match has been made. Collect the *Response Cards* from the students.

Follow-Up:

At the conclusion of the activity, have the students respond to the following:

> **Without mentioning any names, talk about a time you or someone you know was left out of a group.**

WALLOPING WARTHOG
THREATENING

Purpose:

To help students practice dealing with threats and understand when to get help

Grade Levels: 1-3

Materials Needed:

For The Leader:

☐ *Walloping Warthog Hat* (pages 208-211)
☐ Chalkboard and chalk

Pre-Lesson Preparation:

If not constructed previously, make the *Walloping Warthog Hat* according to its directions.

Optional: Prior to presenting the lesson, write the four steps in handling bullies (see page 65) on the chalkboard.

Lesson:

Optional: Pick one or two of the previously taught bully songs to review. If the songs are part of this presentation, write the following words on the chalkboard:

RUN, RUN

Run, Run. Tell an adult.
Run, Run. Tell an adult.
Run, Run. Tell an adult.
Tell an adult right now.

A bully's in my classroom, shoo her away.
A bully's in my classroom, shoo him away.
A bully's in my classroom, shoo her away.
Shoo them away right now.

Then tell the children:

Today we will learn the song *Run, Run.* **We will sing it to the tune of** *Skip To My Lou.* **How many of you have heard or know that song?** (Pause for responses.) **Can anyone sing one verse for us?** (Allow one or more students to sing a verse of *Skip To My Lou.*)

Help the students with any new words in *Run, Run.* Practice the words of the new song, line by line, with the class. Have the students repeat each line to you. Then have the students sing the song.

Introduce or continue the lesson by saying:

Some bullies are dangerous and will threaten you.

Then ask the following questions:

What might a bully say or do that would threaten someone? (A bully might say, "I'm going to beat you up" or "I'm going to hit (push, choke) you." Accept any other appropriate answers.)

What is the safest way to deal with a bully who acts like a mean warthog? (Get help from an adult. Have a buddy with you at all times.)

Introduce or review the four steps in handling bullies. Write the following four steps on the chalkboard:

1. Be alert! Recognize a bully's actions or words.

2. Confront the bully. Tell the bully what he/she said or did.

3. Confirm what the bully is doing or talk with others about it. What can you say to others who are witnesses?

4. Support and help others. Be there for others if they are being bullied.

Then say:

These are the four ways you can deal with a bully who is threatening you.

Continue the lesson by saying aloud or writing on the chalkboard examples of what students could say to a bully who threatens them. Discuss the examples.

1. Be alert! Recognize a bully's actions or words. Stay away from people who may hurt you. If you cannot avoid the bully, be sure to have a friend with you. Don't say anything. Just leave.

2. Confront the bully. Tell the bully what he/she said or did. Say, "You threatened me."

3. Confirm what the bully is doing or talk with others about it. What can you say to others who are witnesses? Ask, "Did he/she just threaten me?"

4. Support and help others. Be there for others if they are being bullied. Say, "Don't hurt him/her or I'll tell."

Game Procedure:

Continue the lesson by explaining the game procedure. Say:

Today we are going to practice dealing with bullies who threaten you. I will choose six people to come to the front of the room. I will choose one other person to be the *warthog* and wear the *Walloping Warthog Hat*. The person wearing the hat will go up to each of the six people and grunt like a mean warthog or oink like a harmless pig. If the *warthog* oinks, the person should do nothing. If the *warthog* grunts and says something threatening, the person must either:

Say nothing and walk away.

Ask the teacher to join him or her, then say to the *warthog*, "You threatened me."

Turn to the class and ask, "Did he (she) just threaten me?"

If one of the six people in the front of the room does nothing when the *warthog* grunts or responds to an oink as if it is threatening, that person will be asked to sit down. Then I will choose another student from the class to replace him or her. At that time, I will also choose a new *warthog*.

If all six people respond correctly to the *warthog*, we'll applaud their success in responding to a threatening situation. That group will retire, and a new group of six can come to the front of the room as well as a new *warthog*.

Please remember this is only role-playing. No one should try to intentionally hurt another person's feelings. No touching is allowed. Are there any questions?

Select a student to be the *warthog* and six students to come to the front of the room. Play the game until the allotted time has elapsed.

Follow-Up:

At the conclusion of the activity, have the students respond to the following:

Tell when it is not safe to confront a threatening bully.

Other than what we learned today, what ways would be safe to confront a threatening bully?

![palm tree] TYRANNICAL TIGER
MY WAY OR NO WAY

Purpose:

To help students learn to recognize someone who is bossy and develop skills to deal positively with that person

Grade Levels: 2-5

Materials Needed:

For The Leader:

☐ *Tyrannical Tiger Hat* (pages 212-216)
☐ Chalkboard and chalk

Pre-Lesson Preparation:

If not constructed previously, make the *Tyrannical Tiger Hat* according to its directions.

Optional: Prior to presenting the lesson, write the four steps in handling bullies (see page 68) on the chalkboard.

Lesson:

Optional: Pick one or two of the previously taught bully songs to review. If the songs are part of this presentation, write the following words on the chalkboard:

BULLY, DON'T BOTHER ME

Bully, don't bother me.
Bully, don't bother me.
Bully, don't bother me,
'Cause I am a SOMEBODY!

(*Note:* If the game *Peek-A-Boo Bully* has already been presented, the song *Bully, Don't Bother Me* will have already been learned.)

Then tell the children:

Today we will sing the song *Bully, Don't Bother Me* **to the tune of** *Shoo-Fly Don't Bother Me.* **How many of you have heard or know that song?** (Pause for responses.) **Can anyone sing one verse for us?** (Allow one or more students to sing a verse of *Shoo-Fly Don't Bother Me.*)

Help the students with any new words in *Bully, Don't Bother Me.* Practice the words of the new song, line by line, with the class. Have the students repeat each line to you. Then have the students sing the song.

Introduce or continue the lesson by saying:

Today we are going to learn how to recognize someone who is bossy a lot of the time and learn the best way to handle this type of bully. (Hold up the Tyrannical Tiger Hat.) **This is Tyrannical Tiger. People who are tyrannical are called** *tyrants.* **Tyrants are controlling and always want their own way. One way they get their own way is by bossing others around.**

Then ask the following question:

How do you think Tyrannical Tiger might act around others? (Tyrannical Tiger might want his/her way all of the time, might not share, pouts if he/she doesn't get his/her own way, yells, won't play if things don't go his/her way, etc.)

Introduce or review the four steps in handling bullies. Write the following four steps on the chalkboard:

1. Be alert! Recognize a bully's actions or words.

2. Confront the bully. Tell the bully what he/she said or did.

3. Confirm what the bully is doing or talk with others about it. What can you say to others who are witnesses?

4. Support and help others. Be there for others if they are being bullied.

Then say:

These are the four ways you can deal with a bossy bully.

Continue the lesson by saying aloud or writing on the chalkboard examples of what students could say to a bully who is bossy. Discuss the examples after each strategy.

1. Be alert! Recognize a bully's actions or words. Ask, "What did you say?" to let the bully know that you recognize his/her behavior.

2. Confront the bully. Tell the bully what he/she said or did. Say, "Hey, you're acting bossy," to let the bully know that you know exactly what is happening.

3. Confirm what the bully is doing or talk with others about it. What can you say to others who are witnesses? Ask, "Do you think he/she is being bossy?"

4. Support and help others. Be there for others if they are being bullied. Say, "Don't treat him/her that way."

Game Procedure:

Continue the lesson by explaining the game procedure. Say:

I will send three students out of the room to wait just outside the door for a minute. I will choose one of those three students to be the *Tyrannical Tiger*. Only those three students will know whom I choose to be the *Tyrannical Tiger*. When they come back into the room, you will try to guess which one is the *Tyrannical Tiger*.

When the three players come back into the room, the rest of you will pretend to be working on a project with them or pretend to be playing with them. During the role-play, you will take turns raising your hands to ask one of the three students a question about what you are pretending to do with him or her.

After the question has been answered, someone else may ask one of the other three students the same question or a different question.

Before we begin, let's practice several questions that you might ask. (Help the students ask questions pertaining to the pretend activity, such as, "Would you share a crayon with me?")

At the end of a short questioning time, I will ask you to vote for the student you think is the *Tyrannical Tiger*. When I say, "Vote now," hold up one finger for Player #1, (<u>NAME OF STUDENT</u>); two fingers for Player #2, (<u>NAME OF STUDENT</u>); and three fingers for Player #3, (<u>NAME OF STUDENT</u>). Then I will tell you which student actually is the *Tyrannical Tiger*.

The person pretending to be the *Tyrannical Tiger* may now wear the *Tyrannical Tiger Hat* and say something that *Tyrannical Tiger* might say to someone. When this happens, look at the ways to handle bossy bullies written on the chalkboard. Then decide what answer you would give. I will call on several students to share their answers.

At the end the first round, we will begin a new round with three new people. Everyone will not get a chance to be one of the three students leaving the room, but each of you may have a turn at being a questioner. Are there any questions?

Select the three students and leave the room with them. Choose one of them to be the *Tyrannical Tiger*. Tell the student chosen to be the *Tyrannical Tiger* to act like a tyrant (bossy, always wanting his/her own way) when asked questions by the other students. Tell the other two students to respond to the questions politely. Return to the room and begin the game. Play as many rounds as time allows.

(*Note:* For older students, you may tell the three students waiting outside the room that although only one of them is the *Tyrannical Tiger*, the others may portray a different kind of bully. If you are doing this, explain to the students that more than one bully may be portrayed, but that they are only to identify the one who is bossy.)

Follow-Up:

At the conclusion of the activity, have the students respond to the following:

What can you do if someone is being bossy? (Elicit ideas such as letting the teacher know about the situation; telling the person to stop being bossy; with adult permission, partnering with another person or group; continuing to work with the students who are not bossy, etc.)

How do you feel when someone is being bossy?

ZANY ZEBRA
DENYING DOING WRONG

Purpose:

To help students recognize when a bully accuses others falsely

Grade Levels: 1-3

Materials Needed:

For The Leader:

☐ *Zany Zebra Hat* (pages 217-221)
☐ Black construction paper
☐ Scissors
☐ Copy of *Zany Zebra Statements* (page 172)
☐ Chalkboard and chalk

For Each Student:

☐ Copy of the song *If Bully* (page 157, optional)

Pre-Lesson Preparation:

If not constructed previously, make the *Zany Zebra Hat* according to its directions.

Cut 1" x 6" black stripes out of black construction paper.

Make a copy of the *Zany Zebra Statements*. Cut apart the strips and laminate them for durability.

If you are using the song, make a copy for each student.

Optional: Prior to presenting the lesson, write the four steps in handling bullies (see page 72) on the chalkboard.

Lesson:

(*Note:* If the game *Bully Spy* has been presented, the students will have already learned the *If Bully* song.)

Then say:

Today we will sing the song *If Bully* to the tune of *If You're Happy And You Know It.*

If the students do not know the *If Bully* song, ask:

How many of you have heard or know that song? (Pause for responses.) **Can anyone sing one verse for us?** (Allow one or more students to sing a verse of *If You're Happy And You Know It.* Help the students with any new words in *If Bully.* Practice the words of the new song, line by line, with the class. Have the students repeat each line to you.)

Have the students sing *If Bully.*

Introduce or continue the lesson by saying:

Today's lesson is about bullies who accuse other people of doing something wrong when it was really they themselves who are at fault. This kind of bully is a *Zany Zebra*. (Hold up the Zany Zebra Hat.)

Introduce or review the four steps in handling bullies. Write the following four steps on the chalkboard:

1. Be alert! Recognize a bully's actions or words.

2. Confront the bully. Tell the bully what he/she said or did.

3. Confirm what the bully is doing or talk with others about it. What can you say to others who are witnesses?

4. Support and help others. Be there for others if they are being bullied.

Then say:

These are the four ways you can deal with a bully who is denying doing anything wrong.

Continue the lesson by saying aloud or writing on the chalkboard examples of what students could say to a bully who is denying doing anything wrong. Discuss the examples after each strategy.

1. Be alert! Recognize a bully's actions or words. Ask, "What did you say?" or say, "That doesn't sound right."

2. Confront the bully. Tell the bully what he/she said or did. Say, "Hey! That doesn't sound like the truth!" or "That doesn't make sense."

3. Confirm what the bully is doing or talk with others about it. What can you say to others who are witnesses? Ask, "Is that the truth?" or "Did you see what he/she did?"

4. Support and help others. Be there for others if they are being bullied. Say, "Don't say that when you know it's not true."

Game Procedure:

Continue the lesson by explaining the game procedure. Say:

I will divide you into small teams of three to four members. Choose one person in your group to role-play the *Zany Zebra*. A *Zany Zebra* doesn't admit the truth or does not believe he or she has done anything wrong. Each team will take a turn responding to a statement read by its team member who is role-playing the *Zany Zebra*. (If the student cannot read the words, the leader should whisper the words to the student and have him/her say them aloud.) **For each new round, a new *Zany Zebra* can be chosen for each team.**

If the team members help each other respond to *Zany Zebra* in a way that we've practiced, that team will earn a black zebra stripe. The team with the most zebra stripes can give us a *neigh* at the end of the activity. Hopefully, everyone will be a winner.

Are there any questions?

Divide the class into groups of three or four students. Tell each group to choose one of its team members to be the *Zany Zebra*. Select one group to begin and ask that group to come to the front of the room. Place the *Zany Zebra Hat* on the student chosen to be the group's *Zany Zebra*. Instruct the *Zany Zebra* to choose a *Zany Zebra Statement* and read it aloud. If the other group members respond with an appropriate technique, they earn a zebra stripe. After the first group has finished, continue the game with the next group.

Follow-Up:

At the conclusion of the activity, have the students respond to the following:

What helped you respond to the *Zany Zebra*?

How would you feel if you were wrongly accused of something?

ERUPTING ELEPHANT
PUT-DOWNS

Purpose:

To help students to recognize put-downs

Grade Levels: 1-3

Materials Needed:

For The Leader:

- [ ] *Erupting Elephant Hat* (pages 222-226)
- [ ] Copy of *Erupting Elephant Cards* (pages 173-174)
- [ ] Chalkboard and chalk

For Each Student:

- [ ] Copy of the song *The Bully In The School* (page 151, optional)

Pre-Lesson Preparation:

If not constructed previously, make the *Erupting Elephant Hat* according to its directions.

Make a copy of the *Erupting Elephant Cards*. Cut apart the cards and laminate them for durability.

If you are using the song, make a copy for each student.

Optional: Prior to presenting the lesson, write the four steps in handling bullies (see page 75) on the chalkboard.

Lesson:

Optional: If the songs are part of your presentation, distribute *The Bully In The School* lyric sheet to each student. (*Note:* If the *Spot The Bully* lesson has been presented, the students will have already learned *The Bully In The School* song.)

Then say:

Today we will sing the song *The Bully In The School* to the tune of *The Farmer In The Dell*.

If the students do not know *The Bully In The School* song, say:

How many of you have heard or know the song *The Farmer In The Dell*? (Pause for responses.) **Can anyone sing one verse for us?** (Allow one or more students to sing a verse of *The Farmer In The Dell*. Help the students with any new words in *The Bully In The School*. Practice the words of the new song, line by line, with the class. Have the students repeat each line to you.)

Have the students sing *The Bully In The School*.

Introduce or continue the lesson by saying:

Today we are going to look at another jungle animal that reminds us of a bully. That animal is the elephant. If an elephant sat on top of you, that would be a very tragic situation. Bullies may not sit on you, but they can say put-downs or things that leave you feeling worthless or sad. That is also tragic. Without using any names, what are some put-downs you have heard? (Pause for student responses. Examples could be: Your hair looks awful. Your nose is too big. Four Eyes. Your mother is fat.)

These are the four ways you can deal with a bully who is putting someone down.

Introduce or review the four steps in handling bullies. Write the following four steps on the chalkboard:

1. Be alert! Recognize a bully's actions or words.

2. Confront the bully. Tell the bully what he/she said or did.

3. Confirm what the bully is doing or talk with others about it. What can you say to others who are witnesses?

4. Support and help others. Be there for others if they are being bullied.

Continue the lesson by saying aloud or writing on the chalkboard examples of what students could say to a bully who uses put-downs. Discuss the examples after each strategy.

1. Be alert! Recognize a bully's actions or words. Say, "I can't believe you said that," or "That doesn't make good sense," or "That sounds like a bully."

2. Confront the bully. Tell the bully what he/she said or did. Say, "That was a put-down!" or ask, "Bullies use put-downs. Are you a bully?"

3. Confirm what the bully is doing or talk with others about it. What can you say to others who are witnesses? Ask your friends, "Is that the truth?"

4. Support and help others. Be there for others if they are being bullied. Say, "Don't say that. It's mean."

Game Procedure:

Continue the lesson by explaining the game procedure. Say:

In this game, we're going to make a train. I'll choose someone to be the engineer at the front of the train. That person can wear the *Erupting Elephant Hat*. The *elephant engineer* will also hold the deck of *Erupting Elephant Cards*. The *elephant engineer* will tap someone in the class on the shoulder. That person will draw an *Erupting Elephant Card* and read it aloud. (If the student cannot read the words, the leader should whisper the words to the student and have him/her say them aloud.) **If the *Erupting Elephant Card* says something that shows good manners, the person tapped may hook onto the train by standing behind the *elephant engineer* and placing his or her hands on the *engineer's* shoulders. If the *Erupting Elephant Card* is a put-down, everyone, including the person who just read the card, must quickly sit down on the floor.**

The student who sits down first qualifies to become the new *elephant engineer*, because he or she was the first person to recognize the put-down. The game then continues with the new *elephant engineer*. Are there any questions?

Choose a student to be the *elephant engineer* and give him/her the deck of cards. Begin the game. Play as many rounds as time allows.

Follow-Up:

At the conclusion of the activity, have the students respond to the following:

How do put-down statements leave you feeling? Why?

What are some good positive comeback statements that you can make if someone puts you down? (That's not your business. Give me a break. When I need your opinion, I'll ask for it. What? What? I can't hear you. That's a very strange comment. I'll run that by our teacher.)

GLOATING GIRAFFE
ACTING AS IF YOU ARE BETTER THAN OTHERS

Purpose:

To help students learn ways to deal with people who act as if they are better than others

Grade Levels: 3-5

Materials Needed:

For The Leader:

☐ *Gloating Giraffe Hat* (pages 227-231)
☐ Chalkboard and chalk

Pre-Lesson Preparation:

If not constructed previously, make the *Gloating Giraffe Hat* according to its directions.

Optional: Prior to presenting the lesson, write the four steps in handling bullies (see page 78) on the chalkboard.

Lesson:

Optional: If the songs are part of your presentation, have the students sing a few of the bully songs they learned in previous lessons. If the children have not learned any of the songs, choose one or more songs from other lessons.

Introduce or continue the lesson by saying:

(*Note:* If this is not the first lesson from this program, begin with this statement. If it is the first lesson, skip this sentence and begin with the next paragraph.) **We have been studying different kinds of bullies. Who can remember some of the types of bullies we have discussed?** (Pause for student responses. Accept names of the jungle animals, and, if necessary, remind the students what type of bully each animal represents.)

Today we will look at the giraffe, with its long neck. The giraffe's nose is up in the air, and it doesn't even know or care if we exist. Some bullies act that way,

too. They always overlook other people, don't listen to them, act as if they think they are better than others, gloat because they think they are better than everyone, and leave people out.

These are the four ways you can deal with bullies who think they are better than other people.

Introduce or review the four steps in handling bullies. Write the following four steps on the chalkboard:

1. Be alert! Recognize a bully's actions or words.

2. Confront the bully. Tell the bully what he/she said or did.

3. Confirm what the bully is doing or talk with others about it. What can you say to others who are witnesses?

4. Support and help others. Be there for others if they are being bullied.

Continue the lesson by saying aloud or writing on the chalkboard examples of what students could say to a bully who thinks he/she is better than other people. Discuss the examples after each strategy.

1. Be alert! Recognize a bully's actions or words. Ask, "What did you say?" or say, "I can't believe you did that."

2. Confront the bully. Tell the bully what he/she said or did. Ask, "Did you mean to leave me out?" or say, "Hey! I was talking! It's my turn," or "I can't play with you if you are going to treat me that way."

3. Confirm what the bully is doing or talk with others about it. What can you say to others who are witnesses? Ask, "Do you think he/she just left me out?"

4. Support and help others. Be there for others if they are being bullied. Say, "Don't do that to her/him."

Game Procedure:

Continue the lesson by explaining the game procedure. Say:

We are going to practice ways to deal with a person who leaves someone out of a group or conversation. When that happens, the person being left out needs to find a new group or person to play with.

I will choose four (or six or any other multiple of two, depending on the number of students in the class and how many rounds you wish to play) people to come forward and stand in the front of the room. The students chosen will form pairs. Each pair should stand about two feet from the next pair. The partners should face each other, standing about two feet apart. (Choose the students and have them form pairs in the front of the room.)

Now, I will choose one student to come to the front of the room, role-play the *giraffe,* and wear the *Gloating Giraffe Hat.* (Choose the *giraffe.*)

To begin the game, the *giraffe* will go from paired group to paired group, whispering, "Don't let the *mover* into your group. You are too good for the *mover,*" then stand with his or her back to the group. Then each group must quietly decide whether they will let the *mover* in. Once you reach a decision, you cannot change your choice. (Have the giraffe whisper to each group. Allow time for the groups to decide whether they will let the *mover* in.)

I will now choose another student to be the *mover.* (Choose the *mover. Note:* Do not choose a student with peer relationship problems to be the mover.) When I call out "Move!" the *mover* will move to each paired group and ask, "May I Play?" If the pair pulls the *mover* between them, then the *mover* is safe. If the pair turns and stands back to back, the *mover* must quickly try to join another pair. When I call out "Move!" the *giraffe* must count to five before trying to catch the *mover.* The *giraffe* has 30 seconds to try to catch the *mover* before the *mover* gets to a safe pair. There can be no running, and the *giraffe* must wear the hat at all times.

After the *mover* has contacted each of the pairs or the *giraffe* has caught the *mover,* the round is over. New students will be chosen for the next round. Are there any questions?

Begin the game. Play as many rounds as time allows.

Follow-Up:

Have the students portraying the *mover* respond to the following:

How did you feel when you were left out of a group?

How did you feel when a group pulled you in to join it?

Have the students in the pairs respond to the following:

How did you decide whether to let the *mover* into your group?

How did you feel when you excluded the *mover* from your group?

How did you feel when you included the *mover* in your group?

MENACING MONKEY
STAYING SAFE IN UNSAFE SITUATIONS

Purpose:

To help students understand how to be safe in an unsafe situation

Grade Levels: 3-5

Materials Needed:

For The Leader:

- [ ] *Menacing Monkey Hat* (pages 232-236)
- [ ] 2 chalkboard erasers
- [ ] Watch with a second hand

Pre-Lesson Preparation:

If not constructed previously, make the *Menacing Monkey Hat* according to its directions.

Lesson:

Optional: If the songs are part of your presentation, have the students sing a few of the bully songs they learned in previous lessons. If the children have not learned any of the songs, choose one or more songs from other lessons.

Introduce or continue the lesson by saying:

Today we will be learning about how to handle a bully. Who can tell me about times when you need a buddy? (Pause for responses. Examples are: swimming, hiking, on a playground, in a public restroom, etc.) **Why would you need a buddy at these times?** (For safety, companionship, fun, etc.) **Buddies are very important at school, too. You need to stay with your friends for safety when you are around a bully, especially since bullies and their friends tend to gang up on others.**

Game Procedure:

Continue the lesson by explaining the game procedure. Say:

Our game today is called *Menacing Monkey*. I will choose one person to be the *monkey bully* and ask him or her to wear the *Menacing Monkey Hat*. I will choose another person to be someone who doesn't have a buddy. This person will be the *monkey bully's* victim. Both the *monkey bully* and the *victim* will balance a chalkboard eraser on their shoulders. The eraser must stay on their shoulders throughout the chase. A player who feels the eraser falling may stop and read-just the eraser so it is balanced, then continue the game. If the eraser falls to the floor, the player must stop, pick it up, place it on his or her shoulder, then continue the game. (*Note:* If balancing an eraser on their shoulders seems too diffi-cult, students may hold the eraser on their shoulders while walking around the room.) It is the job of the *monkey bully* to try and tag the *victim* while both are walking around the room, weaving in and out between the desks.

The *victim* must to try to tap three buddies for help. The *buddies* will try to form a circle to protect the *victim* from being tagged by the *monkey bully*. Remember: Players must walk. No running is allowed.

The *monkey bully* can tag only the *victim*. If the *monkey bully* tags someone else, play stops immediately, and the *monkey bully* loses the game. Then I will choose a new *monkey bully*. The other players will remain in the game for an-other round.

The entire game lasts 30 seconds. In that time, the *monkey bully* must try to tag the *victim,* the *victim* tries to tap three other players to serve as *buddies*, and the *buddies* try to circle the *victim* in order to keep the *monkey bully* away.

Once the 30 seconds are up, we'll see if the *monkey bully* was successful in tagging the *victim* or if the *victim* was protected by the *buddies*.

Then new players will be chosen. If the person gets tagged, the *monkey bully* may choose to become the *victim* and play another round.

Are there any questions?

Choose the two players and begin the game.

Follow-Up:

At the conclusion of the activity, have the students respond to the following:

When confronted by bullies, how important is the buddy system? Why?

How do you think someone with buddy protection would feel? How would a person feel without buddy protection?

What are some places at school where unsafe situations could occur?

What are some places in a neighborhood where unsafe situations could occur?

HARASSING HIPPO
NAME-CALLING

Purpose:

To give students practice in dealing with name-calling

Grade Levels: 3-5

Materials Needed:

For The Leader:

☐ *Harassing Hippo Hat* (pages 237-240)
☐ Copy of *Harassing Hippo Cards* (pages 175-176)
☐ Two non-working or play telephones (optional)
☐ Chalkboard and chalk

Pre-Lesson Preparation:

If not constructed previously, make the *Harassing Hippo Hat* according to its directions.

Make a copy of the *Harassing Hippo Cards*. Cut apart the cards and laminate them for durability.

Optional: Prior to presenting the lesson, write the four steps in handling bullies (see page 84) on the chalkboard.

Lesson:

Optional: If the songs are part of your presentation, have the students sing a few of the bully songs they learned in previous lessons. If the children have not learned any of the songs, choose one or more songs from other lessons.

Introduce or continue the lesson by saying:

Without using any names, tell me the kinds of bullies that you have noticed at school. (If this is not the first lesson, elicit the characteristics of the jungle animals that have been introduced.)

Introduce or review the four steps in handling bullies. Write the following four steps on the chalkboard:

1. Be alert! Recognize a bully's actions or words.

2. Confront the bully. Tell the bully what he/she said or did.

3. Confirm what the bully is doing or talk with others about it. What can you say to others who are witnesses?

4. Support and help others. Be there for others if they are being bullied.

Then say:

These are the four ways you can deal with a bully who is name-calling.

Continue the lesson by saying aloud or writing on the chalkboard examples of what students could say to a bully who is name-calling. Discuss the examples after each strategy.

1. Be alert! Recognize a bully's actions or words. Ask, "What did you say?" or say, "That's name-calling," or "That's sounding like a bully."

2. Confront the bully. Tell the bully what he/she said or did. Ask, "Did you mean to call me that?" or say, "That makes no sense," or "I'm leaving until you can talk with good manners."

3. Confirm what the bully is doing or talk with others about it. What can you say to others who are witnesses? Ask, "Did you just hear that? We might have to tell an adult!"

4. Support and help others. Be there for others if they are being bullied. What can we do or say on behalf of a friend who is bullied? Say, "Don't say that. It's mean/rude."

Game Procedure:

Continue the lesson by explaining the game procedure. Say:

In this game, two people will pretend to be talking on telephones. (If telephones are unavailable, the students will pretend to be using telephones.) **One student will be the** *caller*, **and wear the** *Harassing Hippo Hat*. **The other student will be the** *listener*. **I will give the** *caller* **a** *Harassing Hippo Card*. (*Note:* To avoid embarrassing or unintentionally hurting a student's feelings, be sure what is written on the card is *not* a trait the *listener* possesses.) **If the card has a picture of a happy hippopotamus, the** *caller* **should "talk" on the telephone in a positive way to the** *listener* **about school activities, interests, etc. If the card has a picture of a** *Harassing Hippopotamus* **on it, the** *caller* **must read the words written on the card to the other person on the telephone. The cards are printed with examples of negative, name-calling statements. These examples are not as rude as some names people are actually called. Remember: Name-calling is a put-down. Bullies put other people down.**

The *caller* **begins the round by saying "Ring, Ring!" The other person will then "answer" the telephone and listen to the** *caller*. **If the** *caller* **is mannerly and positive, the** *listener* **should respond in a friendly way. If the** *caller* **sounds like a bully, the** *listener* **should deal positively with the** *caller* **by using one of the ways to handle a bully that we have just discussed.**

After a minute of conversation, new students will be chosen to play our game.

Are there any questions?

Choose the two players. Begin the game.

Follow-Up:

At the conclusion of the activity, have the students who were *listeners* respond to the following:

How did you feel when the *caller* **called you names?**

Was it difficult or easy to handle the name-caller? Why or why not?

REFUSING RHINO
DENYING, LYING

Purpose:

To teach students to protect themselves from a bully who is lying or denying any wrongdoing

Grade Levels: 3-5

Materials Needed:

For The Leader:

- [ ] *Refusing Rhino Hat* (pages 241-244)
- [ ] Copy of *Refusing Rhino Statements* (page 177)
- [ ] 2 copies of *Refusing Rhino Cards* (page 178)
- [ ] 4 pieces of posterboard
- [ ] Black marker
- [ ] Chalkboard and chalk

Pre-Lesson Preparation:

If not constructed previously, make the *Refusing Rhino Hat* according to its directions.

Make two sets of the *Refusing Rhino Cards*. Cut apart the cards and laminate them for durability.

Make a copy of the *Refusing Rhino Statements.*

Using posterboard, make four signs printed with the following words to display in the classroom:

1. Spot The Bully Station
2. Confront Station
3. Confirm Team Station
4. Help Station

Optional: Prior to presenting the lesson, write the four steps in handling bullies (see page 87) on the chalkboard.

Lesson:

Optional: If the songs are part of your presentation, have the students sing a few of the bully songs they learned in previous lessons. If the children have not learned any of the songs, choose one or more songs from other lessons.

Introduce or continue the lesson by saying:

Today we will learn to recognize people who lie to protect themselves.

Introduce or review the four steps in handling bullies. Write the following four steps on the chalkboard:

1. Be alert! Recognize a bully's actions or words.

2. Confront the bully. Tell the bully what he/she said or did.

3. Confirm what the bully is doing or talk with others about it. What can you say to others who are witnesses?

4. Support and help others. Be there for others if they are being bullied.

Then say:

These are the four ways you can deal with a bully who is lying or denying any wrongdoing.

Continue the lesson by saying aloud or writing on the chalkboard examples of what students could say to a bully who is lying. Discuss the examples after each strategy.

1. Be alert! Recognize a bully's actions or words. Ask, "What did you say?" or say, "That's lying," or "You sound like a bully."

2. Confront the bully. Tell the bully what he/she said or did. Ask, "Did you mean to call me that?" or say, "That makes no sense," or "I'm leaving until you can tell the truth."

3. Confirm what the bully is doing or talk with others about it. What can you say to others who are witnesses? Ask, "Did you hear that? We might have to tell an adult!"

4. Support and help others. Be there for others if they are being bullied. What can we do or say on behalf of a friend who is bullied? Say, "Don't say that. It's a lie!"

Game Procedure:

Continue the lesson by explaining the game procedure. Say:

In this game, there will be four stations in the room. I'll put a sign at each station. (As you go around the room, identify each station, and display the sign.)

The back right corner of the room will be the *Spot The Bully Station*. The front right corner of the room will be the *Confront Station*. The back left corner will be the *Confirm Team Station*, and the front left corner will be the *Help Station*. These stations represent the ways of dealing with bullies that we have discussed.

I will choose four people to be the *refusing rhinos*. One will be the head of the pack and will wear the *Refusing Rhino Hat*. Each *refusing rhino* will earn a *Refusing Rhino Card* if he or she is at the correct station by the time the class and I count slowly to 10. Each card your group collects is worth one point.

To decide which station is correct, I will first read aloud statements that describe ways to deal with bullies who are lying or denying any wrongdoing. If the statement I read sounds like the person being bullied is confronting the bully, the *refusing rhinos* should walk to the *Confront Station*. If the statement I read sounds like the person is recognizing a bully, the *refusing rhinos* should walk to the *Spot The Bully Station*. If the statement I read sounds like a the person is asking for confirmation from others, the *refusing rhinos* should go to the *Confront Team Station*. If the statement sounds like a supporting and helping statement, the *refusing rhinos* should go to the *Help Station*.

Do not run inside the room. You should have plenty of time to make your decision and walk to one of the stations. Not everyone in the group has to go the same station. But once at a station, players cannot move to another station. Remember that each station stands for one way to deal with a bully.

After I read four statements, the students in the first group will count the number of cards they each have collected. I will total the points and write the team's score on the chalkboard. Then I will choose another group of four people to play the game. After everyone has had a chance to participate, the group with the most points will be declared the winner.

Are there any questions?

Choose the four players. Begin the game.

Follow-Up:

At the conclusion of the activity, have the students respond to the following:

What types of statements were easiest to identify with the correct station? Why?

What statements were most difficult to identify with the correct station? Why?

SNAPPY SNAKE
RUDENESS

Purpose:

To help students realize that they are not responsible if someone else is rude or moody

Grade Levels: 3-5

Materials Needed:

For The Leader:

☐ *Snappy Snake Hat* (pages 245-250)
☐ Copy of *Snappy Snake Situation Cards* (pages 180-184)

For Each Student:

☐ Copy of *Snappy Snake* song (page 179, optional)

Pre-Lesson Preparation:

If not constructed previously, make the *Snappy Snake Hat* according to its directions.

Make a copy of the *Snappy Snake Situation Cards*. Cut apart the cards and laminate them for durability.

If songs are part of your presentation, make a copy of *Snappy Snake* for each student.

Optional: Prior to presenting the lesson, write the four steps in handling bullies (see page 90) on the chalkboard.

Lesson:

Optional: If the songs are part of your presentation, distribute the *Snappy Snake* lyric sheet to each student.

Then say:

Today we will begin our lesson by learning a song about a bully. It is called *Snappy Snake* and is sung to the tune of *She'll Be Comin' 'Round The Moun-*

tain. **How many of you have heard or know that song?** (Pause for responses.) **Can anyone sing one verse for us?** (Allow one or more students to sing a verse from *She'll Be Comin' 'Round The Mountain.* Help the students with any new words in *Snappy Snake.* Practice the words of the new song, line by line, with the class. Have the students repeat each line to you.)

Have the students sing *Snappy Snake.*

Introduce or continue the lesson by asking the following questions:

What do you think it means when someone says, "Behave yourself"? (It means use appropriate language; listen; follow directions; be pleasant, not grouchy; etc.)

How do you feel when someone uses bad manners and doesn't behave himself or herself? (Accept all appropriate answers.)

Is it your fault when someone else is grouchy or rude? Why or why not? (No. Acting grouchy or rude is the choice of the person behaving in that manner.)

Introduce or review the four steps in handling bullies. Write the following four steps on the chalkboard:

1. Be alert! Recognize a bully's actions or words.

2. Confront the bully. Tell the bully what he/she said or did.

3. Confirm what the bully is doing or talk with others about it. What can you say to others who are witnesses?

4. Support and help others. Be there for others if they are being bullied.

Then say:

These are the four ways you can deal with a bully who acts rude to you.

Continue the lesson by saying aloud or writing on the chalkboard examples of what students could say to a bully who is rude. Discuss the examples after each strategy.

1. Be alert! Recognize a bully's actions or words. Ask, "What did you say?" or say, "That's rude!" or "You sound like a bully."

2. Confront the bully. Tell the bully what he/she said or did. Say, "That's rude!" or "You are using bad manners."

3. Confirm what the bully is doing or talk with others about it. What can you say to others who are witnesses? Ask, "Do you think that's rude?"

4. Support and help others. Be there for others if they are being bullied. What can we do or say on behalf of a friend who is bullied? Say, "Don't be so rude to him/her!"

Game Procedure:

Continue the lesson by explaining the game procedure. Say:

Today we are going to put on little plays, called *skits*, in which some of you will have parts to read and act out. Each one of you in a group will be given a number.

Divide the students into groups of three members. Assign each person in each group to be Number 1, 2, or 3. Any extra students may serve as the judges.

Then say:

I will assign each group a skit. Your part will be the number in the skit that matches the number you were given. Each of you should read over your parts with your group several times. When doing so, be sure to use good expressions when acting out your part. You will only have three minutes to practice. In the skit, one of you will be a rude, bad-mannered *bully*. Since you do not want the other groups to know who your *bully* is, you must practice very quietly, whispering your lines.

Assign the skits to each group. Then have the groups begin their three-minute practice time. When the allotted time has elapsed, say:

Now we will begin presenting our skits. Remember: One person in each skit will be acting in a rude manner. That person is a bad-mannered *bully*. I will choose another team to be the judges (also include as judges any students not involved in a skit). **After your group presents its skit, the judges will choose which person was the *bully* and tell why they made that choice. The person who is chosen as the *bully* will wear the *Snappy Snake Hat* until the next group's *bully* is chosen.**

Are there any questions?

Proceed with the activity until all the skits have been presented.

Follow-Up:

At the conclusion of the activity, have the students who were judges respond to the following:

What made you notice the *Snappy Snake* in each group?

What can you do or say to this type of bully? (Emphasize the four steps for handling a bully.)

CROAKING CROCODILE
YELLING

Purpose:

To help students learn to confront someone who yells

Grade Levels: 3-5

Materials Needed:

For The Leader:

☐ *Croaking Crocodile Hat* (pages 251-255)

For Each Student:

☐ Drawing Paper
☐ Pencil

Pre-Lesson Preparation:

If not constructed previously, make the *Croaking Crocodile Hat* according to its directions.

Optional: Prior to presenting the lesson, write the four steps in handling bullies (see page 93) on the chalkboard.

Lesson:

Optional: If the songs are part of your presentation, have the students sing a few of the bully songs they learned in previous lessons. If the children have not learned any of the songs, choose one or more songs from other lessons.

Introduce or continue the lesson:

> **Today we will be learning some ways to deal positively with someone who yells at you.**

Introduce or review the four steps in handling bullies. Write the following four steps on the chalkboard:

1. Be alert! Recognize a bully's actions or words.

2. Confront the bully. Tell the bully what he/she said or did.

3. Confirm what the bully is doing or talk with others about it. What can you say to others who are witnesses?

4. Support and help others. Be there for others if they are being bullied.

Then say:

These are the four ways you can deal with a bully who is yelling at you.

Continue the lesson by saying aloud or writing on the chalkboard examples of what students could say to a bully who is yelling. Discuss the examples after each strategy.

1. Be alert! Recognize a bully's actions or words. Say, "That's too loud," or "You sound like a bully."

2. Confront the bully. Tell the bully what he/she said or did. Say, "You're yelling," or "Stop talking so loudly."

3. Confirm what the bully is doing or talk with others about it. What can you say to others who are witnesses? Ask, "Can you hear that yelling?" or say, "Tell her/him to quiet down."

4. Support and help others. Be there for others if they are being bullied. What can we do or say on behalf of a friend who is bullied? Say, "Don't yell at her/him," or "Quiet down!"

Game Procedure:

Continue the lesson by explaining the game procedure. Say:

In today's lesson, *Sound Off, Croaking Crocodile*, I am going to read aloud a story without an ending. You will have a sheet of paper and you can draw a positive picture of the way you think it might end. There is no right or wrong way to end the story. If you want, you may draw it like a cartoon, writing what each character says in a bubble above his or her head. You are to use only a pencil and make your drawings as large as the paper. That way you can hold it up to share with others in the class. When you are showing your drawing to the class, you may wear the *Croaking Crocodile Hat*.

Use your best listening skills as I read the story. In order to do this, your eyes need to look at me as I read. Your hands need to be very still so they don't distract you or bother you, and your mouth needs to be closed so your brain can help you to hear and think clearly about the story.

CONQUERING BULLIES © 2005 MAR✶CO PRODUCTS, INC. 1-800-448-2197

Give each student a piece of drawing paper and a pencil. Then read the following story:

One day at school, a group of (<u>NAME THE GRADE YOU ARE PRESENTING THE LESSON TO</u>) graders went outside with their teacher for a break. They decided to start a ball game and began dividing into teams. One of the players didn't like the team that he/she was on and began yelling to let everyone know what he/she wanted them to do. Now finish the story with a drawing.

Allow two to three minutes for the students to complete their drawings. Then ask the students to share their pictures with the rest of the class. If some children are not quite finished drawing, let them share their pictures anyway. Discuss the effectiveness of the story endings and the positive approaches that were used. Then continue with the following stories, following the same procedure. Give the students more paper when necessary. Continue the activity for as long as time allows.

Other unfinished stories:

The class was looking forward to lunch, since the cafeteria staff had promised there would be a surprise on the menu. Excitedly, the students followed the teacher to the cafeteria to see what it was. To their delight, the cafeteria helpers were wearing costumes that showed the different food groups that are good for everyone to eat. One had a big piece of cheese on her head and wore a yellow outfit; one was dressed in green with leafy stems attached to represent green vegetables; and one of the helpers looked like a chicken drumstick. The students giggled as they went through the line, choosing from all of the food groups. All at once, a student at the back of the line began yelling about how slowly the line was moving. Everyone was just taking time to look at the cafeteria helpers' costumes. Now finish the story with your drawing.

Every time the class lined up to leave the classroom, one of the students, who always wanted to be first, yelled at someone to get out of the way. Now finish the story with your drawing.

Several students from different classrooms were in the restroom. One of the students began to yell at the others about not throwing the paper towels into the trash basket. Everyone was trying to be neat, so the students didn't understand all of this fussing. Now finish the story with your drawing.

Follow-Up:

At the conclusion of the activity, have the students respond to the following:

1. **What do you think is the best way to respond to a yelling bully?**

2. **How can you tell the difference between a person with a loud voice who is not a bully and a person who is yelling and is a bully?**

BULLY STORIES

TWELVE STORY-BASED LESSONS
FOR YOUNGER STUDENTS

Each lesson includes:

A STORY ABOUT THE TYPE OF BULLY FEATURED

DISCUSSION QUESTIONS

ROLE-PLAY ACTIVITY

In each lesson, the children will answer similar questions
about the story read. Each role-play is also similar.
Young children need repetition, and this repetition will enable
them to better grasp the concepts being presented.

LOUD-MOUTH LION
GOSSIPING

Purpose:

To help students relate to a situation in which they are the object of gossip

Grade Levels: K-2

Materials Needed:

For The Leader:

☐ *Loud-Mouth Lion Hat* (pages 198-202)
☐ *Loud-Mouth Lion Story* (pages 99-100)

For Each Student:

☐ Copy of the *Loud-Mouth Lion Story Picture* (optional, page 185)
☐ Crayons or markers (optional)

Pre-Lesson Preparation:

If not constructed previously, make the *Loud-Mouth Lion Hat* according to its directions.

Optional: Make a copy of the *Loud-Mouth Lion Story Picture* for each student.

Lesson:

Introduce the lesson by asking:

What is gossiping? (Elicit the response that *gossiping* is when someone says something untrue or hurtful about another person.)

How would you feel if someone gossiped about you or your family? (Bring out the feelings of being unhappy, hurt, angry, betrayed, etc.)

What does it mean if someone says a person *has a loud mouth*? (The person may have talked too loudly or spread hurtful rumors—in other words, gossiped.)

Before beginning the story, remind the students:

As I read our story, it is important for you to be a good listener. To do this, you must remember to use the parts of your body that help you to be a good listener. Who can tell me what body parts these are and what you should do with them? (Eyes should be facing the reader, hands should be still or in your lap, nose should be pointed toward the reader, mouth is closed, ears are hearing what the reader is saying, brain is thinking about what the reader is saying, and feet and legs are under your desk or crisscrossed.)

Read the *Loud-Mouth Lion Story*.

Discussion Questions:

Ask the students the following questions:

1. **What part of the story do you remember best?** (This does not have to be in sequence, since the part shared is the part most meaningful to the student.)

2. **Why is the lion called Loud-Mouth Lion?** (The lion gossips rather than keeping what he knows to himself. He says things that are not true.)

3. **When the story was over, how did you feel? Why?**

4. **Without using any names, has this type of gossiping ever happened to you?**

5. **What did the story teach you about how to handle a gossiping bully?** (Not to listen to or believe gossip.)

Application:

Tell the students:

I will choose two people to come to the front of the room. One person will wear the *Loud-Mouth Lion Hat*. That person will say, "I'm going to tell everyone about you." Upon hearing that sentence, the other person will respond to the *lion*. What are some things you could say to someone who is acting like a Loud-Mouth Lion? ("Stop saying that." "I'll tell an adult.") **After a response is given, the round will be over. Then two new people will be chosen and we will repeat the activity.**

Optional Activity:

Give each student a copy of the *Loud-Mouth Lion Story Picture* and crayons or markers. Allow the students to color the picture in class or to take it home to color. The pictures may be used as classroom posters.

CONQUERING BULLIES © 2005 MAR✶CO PRODUCTS, INC. 1-800-448-2197

LOUD-MOUTH LION STORY

Once, not long ago, there was a very active little boy who loved to have adventures. His name was Neji. Whenever Neji went out to play, he took his two friends with him. Neji's two faithful friends were: Perty, a colorful parrot, and Skinny Dog Genka, a skinny, scruffy-looking dog. Neji, Perty, and Skinny Dog Genka loved to explore the jungle next to the clearing for Neji's house.

Neji's mother always told him: "Be careful, my son. There are many dangers to watch for in the jungle. Play and have fun, but always protect yourself."

When the three friends strolled off into the jungle to play one day, Loud-Mouth Lion was watching them. Loud-Mouth Lion liked to play games with the three friends. But most of all, what he liked was to tell them things he knew about other animals in the jungle. The only problem was that Loud-Mouth Lion told things that the other animals didn't want told. To get and hold the attention of the animals he was talking to, he would add to the stories things that weren't true. Loud-Mouth Lion was a gossip, and Loud-Mouth Lion was a liar.

Perty, Skinny Dog Genka, and Neji decided to play hide-and-seek. Perty and Skinny Dog Genka went off to hide while Neji covered his eyes and counted to 20. Loud-Mouth Lion watched their every move. He followed Skinny Dog Genka, who was hiding in the bushes. It was a good hiding place, and Neji was looking for him in another direction. Loud-Mouth Lion whispered to Skinny Dog Genka, "What a great hiding place you have! Neji will never find you here." Skinny Dog Genka nodded a *thank you* and kept out of sight in the bushes. "Neji will be surprised that you found such a good hiding place, because he doesn't think you are very smart," Loud-Mouth Lion told Skinny Dog Genka. "Oh, you know, Neji thinks he knows everything. I heard him telling Perty about you the other day. I was surprised. I thought he was your friend." Skinny Dog Genka was hurt. He couldn't believe what he heard. Instead of waiting for Neji to find him, he crept around in the bushes until he could not be seen. Then he went home.

Neji kept looking for Perty and Skinny Dog Genka. Having no luck looking behind the banana trees, Neji turned around and went in the direction where Skinny Dog Genka had been hiding. Meanwhile, Loud-Mouth Lion went over to where Perty was hiding in a hollow stump. "What a great hiding place you have! Neji will never find you here." Perty nodded a *thank you* and wiggled further down into the hollow. "Neji will really be surprised that you found such a good hiding place, because he doesn't think you are very smart," Loud-Mouth Lion told Perty. "You know, he thinks he knows everything. You should have heard what I heard him tell Skinny Dog Genka about you the other day. I was so surprised! I thought he was your friend." Perty was hurt. She couldn't believe what she heard. Instead of waiting for Neji to find her, she worked her way out of the hollow. When she was far enough away so she would not be seen, she flew home.

Neji was alone in the jungle. He became more and more worried, remembering that his mother had always told him to play and have fun, but to protect himself. He began to wonder whether he should forget the game and go home. He called and called to his friends, but they did not answer. Then Loud-Mouth Lion came out from the bushes. "Are you looking for Perty and Skinny Dog Genka?" he asked. "Yes. Have you seen them?" answered Neji. "Of course! They got tired of playing the game and went home," Loud-Mouth Lion replied.

Neji was furious. How could his best friends leave him in the jungle? He raced for home as fast as he could. When he reached the clearing where his house was, he saw Skinny Dog Genka and Perty sitting over at the edge of the jungle. "What's the matter with you?" asked Neji. "You left me in the jungle without saying a word."

"We sure did! Now do you think we aren't smart? We outsmarted you! You kept on looking for us, but we weren't there. Now who is the one who isn't smart?" Perty and Skinny Dog Genka said together.

"What are you talking about?" asked Neji. "Loud-Mouth Lion told me you left because you were tired of playing the game."

"Loud-Mouth Lion? He told us you told him that we weren't very smart," replied Skinny Dog Genka and Perty.

"None of us was very smart," Neji said. "We listened to gossip and lies and it hurt our friendship."

HURTFUL HYENA
LEAVING OTHERS OUT

Purpose:

To help students relate to a situation in which they are left out

Grade Levels: K-2

Materials Needed:

For The Leader:

☐ *Hurtful Hyena Hat* (pages 203-207)
☐ *Hurtful Hyena Story* (page 104)

For Each Student:

☐ Copy of the *Hurtful Hyena Story Picture* (optional, page 186)
☐ Crayons or markers (optional)

Pre-Lesson Preparation:

If not constructed previously, make the *Hurtful Hyena Hat* according to its directions.

Optional: Make a copy of the *Hurtful Hyena Story Picture* for each student.

Lesson:

Introduce the lesson by asking:

What does it mean when someone is *left out* of a group or game? (Elicit the response that being left out of a group or a game is not being included.)

How do you think someone would feel if he or she was left out of a group or a game? (Bring out the feelings of being unhappy, lonely, misused, hurt, angry, etc.)

Before beginning the story, remind the students:

As I read our story, it is important for you to be a good listener. To do this, you must remember to use the parts of your body that help you to be a good listener. Who can tell me what body parts these are and what you should do with them? (Eyes should be facing the reader, hands should be still or in your lap, nose should be pointed toward the reader, mouth is closed, ears are hearing what the reader is saying, brain is thinking about what the reader is saying, and feet and legs are under your desk or crisscrossed.)

Read the *Hurtful Hyena Story.*

Discussion Questions:

Ask the students the following questions:

1. **What part of the story do you remember best?** (This does not have to be in sequence, since the part shared is the part most meaningful to the student.)

2. **When the story was over, how did you feel? Why?**

3. **How does Hurtful Hyena live up to her name in the story?** (She is hurtful when she wants to leave Neji out of the game. When Hurtful Hyena yells because she cannot have her own way, she is a bully.)

4. **The hyena is a hurtful bully. Why is being hurtful a type of bullying behavior?** (A bully doesn't empathize, share, or seem to understand how another person is feeling.)

5. **Without using any names, has this type of bully ever tried to leave you out?**

6. **What did you learn from the story about how to handle a bully?**

Application:

Tell the students:

I will choose two people to come to the front of the room. One person will wear the *Hurtful Hyena Hat*. The person wearing the hat will say, "We don't want to play with you." Upon hearing that sentence, the other person will respond to the *hyena*. What are some things that you could say to someone who is leaving you out? ("You're leaving me out on purpose." "You're acting like a bully." "Did anyone hear what he/she said?") **After a response is given, the round will be over. Then two new people will be chosen and we will repeat the activity.**

Optional Activity:

Give each student a copy of the *Hurtful Hyena Story Picture* and crayons or markers. Allow the students to color the picture in class or to take it home to color. The pictures may be used as classroom posters.

CONQUERING BULLIES © 2005 MAR∗CO PRODUCTS, INC. 1-800-448-2197

HURTFUL HYENA STORY

Neji was playing a game in his yard next to the jungle with his two friends, Perty Parrot and Skinny Dog Genka. Along came Hurtful Hyena. She had a ball and wanted to play, too. That sounded like fun to the three friends, so the four players began their ball game.

Skinny Dog Genka threw the ball into the air. All four players tried to catch it. As the ball came to the ground and bounced on the grass, Neji grabbed it and ran and ran and ran. Perty Parrot squawked and squawked, "Go, Neji! Go, Neji!" Skinny Dog Genka barked and barked, "Give it all you've got, Neji, you're almost to the finish line!" Hurtful Hyena said nothing.

After Neji crossed the finish line, he came back to the group with the ball. Perty Parrot flapped her wings and Skinny Dog Genka jumped up and down. Hurtful Hyena said nothing.

When Neji said, "Let's play again," both Perty Parrot and Skinny Dog Genka were ready to go.

Hurtful Hyena grabbed the ball and began to howl in a shrill, loud voice, "I want the ball. It's mine, and I never get it. Neji, you can't play any more."

Perty Parrot and Skinny Dog Genka could not believe what they were hearing. Hurtful Hyena wanted to leave Neji out because the hyena didn't get her own way.

Neji's feelings were hurt. The friends had been having a good time, but now it was no fun to play with the howling Hurtful Hyena. Then Neji remembered what his mother told him. "Always protect yourself." So Neji decided to tell Hurtful Hyena just what he thought. "Hurtful Hyena, you're not acting like a friend. In fact, you sound like a bully to me."

When Perty Parrot and Skinny Dog Genka heard Neji, they immediately stood up for their friend. Perty Parrot squawked and squawked while Skinny Dog Genka barked and barked.

With everyone against her, Hurtful Hyena stopped her bullying. She knew she was outnumbered.

Now everyone was silent. After a few minutes, Hurtful Hyena howled in a much softer tone of voice, "I didn't mean to sound like a bully. Let's play again. Let's everyone play again."

They all agreed that playing the game with everyone was the most fun, and that no one should be left out.

WALLOPING WARTHOG
THREATENING

Purpose:

To help students relate to a situation in which they are threatened

Grade Levels: K-2

Materials Needed:

For The Leader:

☐ *Walloping Warthog Hat* (pages 208-211)
☐ *Walloping Warthog Story* (page 108)

For Each Student:

☐ Copy of the *Walloping Warthog Story Picture* (optional, page 187)
☐ Crayons or markers (optional)

Pre-Lesson Preparation:

If not constructed previously, make the *Walloping Warthog Hat* according to its directions.

Optional: Make a copy of the *Walloping Warthog Story Picture* for each student.

Lesson:

Introduce the lesson by asking:

Today we are going to hear a story about someone threatening to harm another person. What kinds of things could bullies threaten to do to another person? (Bring out the threats of hurting, kicking, pushing, punching, etc.)

How do you think someone would feel if he or she was threatened? (Bring out the feelings of being afraid, mad, scared, etc.)

Before beginning the story, remind the students:

As I read our story, it is important for you to be a good listener. To do this, you must remember to use the parts of your body that help you to be a good listener. Who can tell me what body parts these are and what you should do with them? (Eyes should be facing the reader, hands should be still or in your lap, nose should be pointed toward the reader, mouth is closed, ears are hearing what the reader is saying, brain is thinking about what the reader is saying, and feet and legs are under your desk or crisscrossed.)

Read the *Walloping Warthog Story.*

Discussion Questions:

Ask the students the following questions:

1. **What part of the story do you remember best?** (This does not have to be in sequence, since the part shared is the part most meaningful to the student.)

2. **When the story was over, how did you feel? Why?**

3. **How do you think Walloping Warthog would have lived up to his name if Perty Parrot and Skinny Dog Genka had not come to Neji's rescue?** (He would have physically hurt Neji.)

4. **Why was Walloping Warthog a bully?** (He was a bully because he threatened Neji and probably would have physically hurt him.)

5. **Without using any names, has this type of bully ever threatened you?**

6. **What did you learn from the story about how to handle a bully?**

Application:

Tell the students:

I will choose two people to come to the front of the room. One person will wear the *Walloping Warthog Hat*. The person wearing the hat will say, "Out of my way!" or I'm going to hurt you." Upon hearing that sentence, the other person will respond to the *warthog*. What are some things you could say to someone who is threatening you? ("You're acting like a bully." "Stop threatening me!" "Did anyone hear that threat?" "I'm going to tell an adult if you don't stop.") **After a response is given, the round will be over. Then two new people will be chosen and we will repeat the activity.**

Optional Activity:

Give each student a copy of the *Walloping Warthog Story Picture* and crayons or markers. Allow the students to color the picture in class or to take it home to color. The pictures may be used as classroom posters.

WALLOPING WARTHOG STORY

Neji and his friends, Perty Parrot and Skinny Dog Genka, went on a scavenger hunt in the jungle. They were looking for different kinds of leaves, pebbles, bird feathers, and anything else that interested their eyes.

Neji carried the basket they were going to fill with their new-found treasures. Perty Parrot flew ahead, using her beady eyes to spot anything that glimmered. Skinny Dog Genka looked for objects by trotting back and forth and scratching lightly at the ground. Neji slowly examined things as high as his head and as low as his toes.

The three friends were happily going through the jungle, adding their treasures to the basket, when Walloping Warthog suddenly jumped in front of Neji. Neji looked around. Perty Parrot and Skinny Dog Genka were nowhere to be seen. Neji was all alone. He had gone too far from safety and now he was in a dangerous spot, out of sight of his house and his friends. There was nowhere to go. The menacing Walloping Warthog was blocking Neji's escape.

Walloping Warthog snorted fiercely and pushed Neji down. Neji was afraid, but he remembered what his mother had said: "Always protect yourself."

Neji yelled as loudly as he could, "STOP IT," and he kept on yelling until his friends, Perty Parrot and Skinny Dog Genka, heard him. Realizing their friend was in trouble, Perty Parrot and Skinny Dog Genka quickly found Neji. Perty Parrot flapped her mighty wings and Skinny Dog Genka growled and barked as they both circled Walloping Warthog.

All this commotion was too much for Walloping Warthog. He took off through the jungle. As he ran away, Walloping Warthog thought to himself, "I will wait for another time to catch Neji by himself."

TYRANNICAL TIGER
BOSSINESS

Purpose:

To teach students how to relate to a situation in which someone is bossy

Grade Levels: K-2

Materials Needed:

For The Leader:

☐ *Tyrannical Tiger Hat* (pages 212-216)
☐ *Tyrannical Tiger Story* (page 112)

For Each Student:

☐ Copy of the *Tyrannical Tiger Story Picture* (optional, page 188)
☐ Crayons or markers (optional)

Pre-Lesson Preparation:

If not constructed previously, make the *Tyrannical Tiger Hat* according to its directions.

Optional: Make a copy of the *Tyrannical Tiger Story Picture* for each student.

Lesson:

Introduce the lesson by asking:

Today we are going to hear a story about a type of bully who is bossy and tells you what to do and must always have his or her own way. What are some other things that bossy bullies do or say? (They do not share objects or take turns, are stubborn about ideas on ways to do things, do not listen to the opinions of others, etc.)

How do you think someone would feel if he or she was bossed around all the time? (Bring out the ideas of being unhappy, ashamed for not sticking up for themselves, not feeling as if they are very smart, etc.)

Our story today is about a tiger who is a tyrant. His name is Tyrannical Tiger. What does the word *tyrannical* mean? (It means being a cruel leader who never cares about the needs of others and only cares about his/her own needs.)

Before beginning the story, remind the students:

As I read our story, it is important for you to be a good listener. To do this, you must remember to use the parts of your body that help you to be a good listener. Who can tell me what body parts these are and what you should do with them? (Eyes should be facing the reader, hands should be still or in your lap, nose should be pointed toward the reader, mouth is closed, ears are hearing what the reader is saying, brain is thinking about what the reader is saying, and feet and legs are under your desk or crisscrossed.)

Read the *Tyrannical Tiger Story.*

Discussion Questions:

Ask the students the following questions:

1. **What part of the story do you remember best?** (This does not have to be in sequence, since the part shared is the part most meaningful to the student.)

2. **When the story was over, how did you feel? Why?**

3. **How did Tyrannical Tiger live up to his name in the story?** (He wanted everything his way. A tyrant dictates what he/she wants and that is what Tyrannical Tiger did.)

4. **Why are the actions of Tyrannical Tiger like those of a bully?** (Tyrannical Tiger was bossy and did not listen to others.)

5. **Without using any names, has this type of bully ever been around you? What happened?**

6. **What did you learn from the story about how to deal with bossy bullies?**

Application:

Tell the students:

> **I will choose two people to come to the front of the room. One person will wear the *Tyrannical Tiger Hat*. The person wearing the hat will say bossy things such as, "Do it this way," "Don't do it that way," or "Do it my way." Upon hearing that sentence, the other person will respond to the *tiger*. What are some things you could say to someone who is bossing you?** ("You're too bossy." "I can't hear you." "Do you think he/she is being bossy?") **After a response is given, the round will be over. Then two new people will be chosen and we will repeat the activity.**

Optional Activity:

Give each student a copy of the *Tyrannical Tiger Story Picture* and crayons or markers. Allow the students to color the picture in class or to take it home to color. The pictures may be used as classroom posters.

TYRANNICAL TIGER STORY

Neji was a very active little boy who loved to have adventures. Every day Neji would take his two friends to explore the jungle next to his house. His faithful friends were, Perty, a colorful parrot, and Skinny Dog Genka, a skinny, scruffy-looking dog.

Neji's mother always told him: "Be careful, my son. There are many dangers to watch for in the jungle. Play and have fun, but always protect yourself."

Neji wanted to build a clubhouse to play in with his friends. Perty began flying around to find some good pieces of wood and logs. Skinny Dog Genka used his huge mouth to carry some of the sticks back to Neji. Neji tugged and pulled the lumber back to the clubhouse site.

After a while, Tyrannical Tiger came along to see what was going on. He watched closely and then began to tell the three friends how to make the clubhouse better. Tyrannical Tiger said, "Pick that up. Put it over there. Put the sticks this way, Now turn the wood that way." The tiger was very bossy.

Soon Neji and his two friends grew very tired of the tiger's bossy ways. There was no doubt about it, the tiger was a bully. It always had to be his way or no way. The three friends never got a chance to build the clubhouse the way they wanted. Each of them felt useless and stupid.

Then Neji remembered what his mother said: "Always protect yourself." And that's what he decided to do.

The next time Tyrannical Tiger told the three hard-working friends what to do as they built the clubhouse, Neji asked him, "What did you say?" When Perty Parrot heard what Neji said, she repeated, "What did you say? What did you say?" This confused the tiger, and he began to think that the three friends might think he was bossy. But he didn't change his bossy ways.

The next time Tyrannical Tiger became bossy, Neji said, "That sounds like a bully," and Perty Parrot repeated, "That sounds like a bully. That sounds like a bully." Tyrannical Tiger said to himself, "I guess they think I am too bossy and that is being a bully." But he didn't change his bossy ways.

When the bossiness continued, Neji asked Perty Parrot and Skinny Dog Genka, "Is this tiger too bossy?" Perty agreed with a "Squawk, Squawk," and Genka growled a loud "Grrr."

Now there was no denying it. Tyrannical Tiger *was* bossy and he *was* a bully and his bossiness *wasn't* going to work. When his bossiness didn't work, Tyrannical Tiger went down the path into the jungle. The three friends continued building their clubhouse together, happy that they had stuck up for each other.

ZANY ZEBRA
DENYING OR LYING
ABOUT DOING THE WRONG THING

Purpose:

To teach students to relate to a situation in which someone denies or lies about a wrongdoing and blames another

Grade Levels: K-2

Materials Needed:

For The Leader:

☐ *Zany Zebra Hat* (pages 217-221)
☐ *Zany Zebra Story* (pages 116-117)

For Each Student:

☐ Copy of the *Zany Zebra Story Picture* (optional, page 189)
☐ Crayons or markers (optional)

Pre-Lesson Preparation:

If not constructed previously, make the *Zany Zebra Hat* according to its directions.

Optional: Make a copy of the *Zany Zebra Story Picture* for each student.

Lesson:

Introduce the lesson by saying:

Today we are going to hear a story about a type of person who does something wrong but won't take the blame for his or her actions. This is the type of bully who does not take responsibility for things he or she has done and might, at times, even blame someone else.

How would you feel if you saw a person do something wrong and then heard that person deny or lie about it? (Bring out the feelings of being surprised, angry, etc., if you get blamed or disciplined instead of the person who did the wrongdoing.)

Before beginning the story, remind the students:

As I read our story, it is important for you to be a good listener. To do this, you must remember to use the parts of your body that help you to be a good listener. Who can tell me what body parts these are and what you should do with them? (Eyes should be facing the reader, hands should be still or in your lap, nose should be pointed toward the reader, mouth is closed, ears are hearing what the reader is saying, brain is thinking about what the reader is saying, and feet and legs are under your desk or crisscrossed.)

Read the story *Zany Zebra Story.*

Discussion Questions:

Ask the students the following questions:

1. **What part of the story do you remember best?** (This does not have to be in sequence, since the part shared is the part most meaningful to the student.)

2. **When the story was over, how did you feel? Why?**

3. **What does it mean to be zany?** (To act silly, outlandish, etc.)

4. **What did Zany Zebra do that made her a bully?** (The zebra blamed others for what she had done and would not take the consequences of her behavior.)

5. **Without using any names, has anyone ever acted like a Zany Zebra toward you? What happened?**

6. **What did you learn from the story about how to deal with bullies like Zany Zebra?**

Application:

Tell the students:

> **I will choose two people to come to the front of the room. One person will wear the *Zany Zebra Hat*. The person wearing the hat will say, "C'mon, I was just joking! Can't you take a joke?" Upon hearing those sentences, the other person will respond to the *zebra*. What are some things you could say to someone who is acting like a Zany Zebra?** ("That's not fair." "That's not funny." "You're acting like a bully when you blame others for something you did." "You must be joking.") **After a response is given, the round will be over. Then two new people will be chosen and we will repeat the activity.**

Optional Activity:

Give each student a copy of the *Zany Zebra Story Picture* and crayons or markers. Allow the students to color the picture in class or to take it home to color. The pictures may be used as classroom posters.

ZANY ZEBRA STORY

One day, Neji invited Zany Zebra to his house to play. Zany Zebra was always a lot of fun at school, making everyone laugh and laugh at her funny antics. Neji was excited about Zany's visit. He had all kinds of games planned and baskets of toys to play with when Zany Zebra arrived.

Zany was excited, too. She loved to play jokes and act silly to get others to laugh and notice her. When Zany arrived, the two friends played a ball game. Zany Zebra ran very fast and Neji caught all of the kicked balls. All except one, that is. That ball sailed through the front window of Neji's house and Neji and Zany heard a loud crash. Neji's mother appeared in the window right away and called out to the ball players: "Who did this to my window?"

Neji looked sheepishly at his mother and said, "I didn't catch the ball that Zany Zebra kicked."

But Zany Zebra ran away, yelling, "I didn't do it! I didn't do it! He did it! He did it!"

Later, after things calmed down and Neji had cleaned up the shattered glass, Zany Zebra returned to play. Neji was disappointed that Zany Zebra had blamed him for the whole accident. And to make it worse, when Neji asked why she ran away, Zany Zebra just laughed and giggled, "I was just playing a joke on you. Can't you take a joke?"

Neji just looked at her. "But you didn't help me clean up the broken glass, and that's not funny," Neji said. "I'm sorry," answered Zany. "Do you want to play some more?"

Neji *did* want to play some more and soon began showing his toys to Zany. The two playmates took out all of the toys, trying different ones and experimenting with others. It wasn't long before they heard Neji's mother call, "Come get lunch." They both dropped everything and ran to the picnic table in the yard.

"Go and pick up all of the toys first," Mother demanded. "What a mess all over the yard!"

Neji headed toward the scattered toys and began putting them into the baskets. But Zany Zebra just kept shaking her head and saying, "I didn't do that. I didn't do that."

No matter how much Neji pleaded for help, Zany refused to budge, denying that she had helped take out any toys at all. Zany even continued playing with toy after toy until Neji took them away and put them in the basket. After all of this commotion, Neji did not enjoy the picnic lunch. He didn't think it was fair that Zany Zebra was enjoying her lunch without having done any work.

Whenever Neji would bring up the subject of not helping pick up the toys, Zany Zebra would just laugh at him and act silly at the table. In fact, Zany was so silly that Neji's mother had to remind them to use good manners. Again, Zany would not admit doing anything wrong. She just pointed to Neji and accused him of doing everything first. "I just followed Neji," Zany said in her most convincing voice. Neji's mother was very disappointed in her son.

When Zany Zebra left that afternoon, Neji decided that he might invite a friend home to play again. But the friend he invited would not be Zany Zebra.

CONQUERING BULLIES © 2005 MAR*CO PRODUCTS, INC. 1-800-448-2197

ERUPTING ELEPHANT
PUTTING OTHERS DOWN

Purpose:

To teach students how to relate to a situation in which someone puts others down

Grade Levels: K-2

Materials Needed:

For The Leader:

☐ *Erupting Elephant Hat* (pages 222-226)
☐ *Erupting Elephant Story* (page 121)

For Each Student:

☐ Copy of the *Erupting Elephant Story Picture* (optional, page 190)
☐ Crayons or markers (optional)

Pre-Lesson Preparation:

If not constructed previously, make the *Erupting Elephant Hat* according to its directions.

Optional: Make a copy of the *Erupting Elephant Story Picture* for each student.

Lesson:

Introduce the lesson by asking:

What does the word *erupting* mean? (It means to explode like a volcano.)

Today we are going to hear a story about a type of person who erupts by putting other people down. What do you think it means to say things that put other people down? (It means to make fun of them, say negative things about them, embarrass them, etc.)

Can you tell some things people might say that would put someone down? ("You can't do anything right." "You're not smart enough." "You never know what to do.")

How would you feel if someone said something to you that put you down? (Bring out the feelings of being sad, ashamed, embarrassed, helpless, etc.)

Before beginning the story, remind the students:

As I read our story, it is important for you to be a good listener. To do this, you must remember to use the parts of your body that help you to be a good listener. Who can tell me what body parts these are and what you should do with them? (Eyes should be facing the reader, hands should be still or in your lap, nose should be pointed toward the reader, mouth is closed, ears are hearing what the reader is saying, brain is thinking about what the reader is saying, and feet and legs are under your desk or crisscrossed.)

Read the *Erupting Elephant Story.*

Discussion Questions:

Ask the students the following questions:

1. **What part of the story do you remember best?** (This does not have to be in sequence, since the part shared is the part most meaningful to the student.)

2. **When the story was over, how did you feel? Why?**

3. **How did Erupting Elephant show that he was a bully?** (The elephant put others down by yelling and calling them names.)

4. **Without using any names, has anyone ever put you down with ugly, untrue statements? What happened?**

5. **What did you learn from the story about how to handle a bully?**

119

Application:

Tell the students:

I will choose two people to come to the front of the room. One person will wear the *Erupting Elephant Hat*. **The person wearing the hat will say, "You don't know anything." Upon hearing that sentence, the other person will respond to the** *elephant.* **What are some things you could say to a bully who puts you down?** ("That's not true." "Leave. You're acting like a bully." "Get a new friend.") **After a response is given, the round will be over. Then two new people will be chosen and we will repeat the activity.**

Optional Activity:

Give each student a copy of the *Erupting Elephant Story Picture* and crayons or markers. Allow the students to color the picture in class or to take it home to color. The pictures may be used as classroom posters.

ERUPTING ELEPHANT STORY

Erupting Elephant was delivering newspapers. His long trunk let him sling the papers into each yard so they landed right next to the front door. Erupting Elephant's huge feet let him cover a lot of territory to get his job done in half the time it took others. Erupting Elephant was a terrific newspaper delivery person. He came down the path, delivering papers, like an express train speeding down a track.

Neji always enjoyed watching Erupting Elephant come down the path to deliver the papers. Although he had never ventured to speak to the elephant, Neji imagined him to be very friendly. After all, anyone who could do the talented things Erupting Elephant could do *must* be friendly. Neji was so sure the elephant was friendly that he didn't stop to wonder why he was called Erupting Elephant.

One day Neji was with his two friends, Perty Parrot and Skinny Dog Genka when Erupting Elephant came to deliver his papers. With his two friends at his side, Neji decided not to be shy and bravely called out, "Hi, Erupting Elephant! May I try to deliver the papers like you?"

Erupting Elephant honked loudly with his trumpet-sounding trunk, "What? Are you kidding? You are too little. You're like a puny mouse with your scrawny arms. Back away!"

Neji couldn't believe what he was hearing. His feelings were very hurt. Perty Parrot and Skinny Dog Genka, seeing their friend upset, immediately tried to come to his rescue. Perty squawked at Erupting Elephant, "Get away! Get away!" while Skinny Dog Genka ran in and out and around Erupting Elephant's big legs, barking.

Erupting Elephant yelled out more put-downs as he tried to keep his balance. "You crazy, ugly bird! You're a birdbrain! Stop that, you sick, mad dog! Get away!" Erupting Elephant was now beginning to show how he got his name.

Neji watched Perty Parrot and Skinny Dog Genka as they confronted Erupting Elephant with their flapping and barking. When Neji heard what Erupting Elephant was saying, he could not believe the words that were coming out of the elephant's mouth. Perty Parrot wasn't crazy or ugly and Skinny Dog Genka was not a sick, mad dog. It was then that Neji also realized that he was certainly not a puny mouse. And that's when he remembered what his mother had said: "Always protect yourself."

Neji knew Erupting Elephant hadn't hurt his body. He was only hurt *inside* his body, where he kept his feelings. But since Erupting Elephant hadn't said anything truthful about him or Perty Parrot or Skinny Dog Genka, Neji chose not to feel sad or put-down because of what Erupting Elephant had said.

Neji, Perty Parrot, and Skinny Dog Genka turned their backs on Erupting Elephant and strolled back to their play area. They forgot about the put-downs that were not true, never were true, and would not be true. Those put-downs deserved no more of their time. As for Erupting Elephant, Neji did not admire him any more.

GLOATING GIRAFFE
BEING SNOOTY

Purpose:

To teach students to relate to a situation in which someone is left out

Grade Levels: K-2

Materials Needed:

For The Leader:

☐ *Gloating Giraffe Hat* (pages 227-231)
☐ *Gloating Giraffe Story* (page 125)

For Each Student:

☐ Copy of the *Gloating Giraffe Story Picture* (optional, page 191)
☐ Crayons or markers (optional)

Pre-Lesson Preparation:

If not constructed previously, make the *Gloating Giraffe Hat* according to its directions.

Optional: Make a copy of the *Gloating Giraffe Story Picture* for each student.

Lesson:

Introduce the lesson by asking:

What does the word *gloat* mean? (It means to show off, boast, act as if you think you are better than others, be snooty, etc.)

Today we are going to hear a story about a type of bully who is snooty. You know the kind of person I mean. The one who thinks he or she is better than other people. Can you tell me some ways people act snooty? (They don't listen to anyone; ignore others; exclude certain people from a group; act as if they are better, smarter, and richer than others; etc.)

**How do you think someone would feel if he or she was left out because some-
one didn't think he or she was good enough to be a part of the group?** (Bring out
the idea of feeling unhappy, lonely, desperate to belong, unworthy, etc.)

Before beginning the story, remind the students:

**As I read our story, it is important for you to be a good listener. To do this, you
must remember to use the parts of your body that help you to be a good listener. Who can tell me what body parts these are and what you should do with
them?** (Eyes should be facing the reader, hands should be still or in your lap, nose
should be pointed toward the reader, mouth is closed, ears are hearing what the reader
is saying, brain is thinking about what the reader is saying, and feet and legs are under
your desk or crisscrossed.)

Read the *Gloating Giraffe Story.*

Discussion Questions:

Ask the students the following questions:

1. **What part of the story do you remember best?** (This does not have to be in
   sequence, since the part shared is the part most meaningful to the student.)

2. **When the story was over, how did you feel? Why?**

3. **What does Gloating Giraffe do to show she is a bully?** (The giraffe acts very
   self-important. She thinks she is better than the others.)

4. **Without using any names, have you
   ever seen a bully acting snooty?
   What happened?**

5. **What did you learn from the story
   about how to handle a bully?**

123

Application:

Tell the students:

> I will choose two people to come to the front of the room. One person will wear the *Gloating Giraffe Hat*. The person wearing the hat will say snooty things such as, "I'm special," "I'm more important than you," or "You're just not good enough to belong to our group." Upon hearing a sentence like that, the other person will respond to the *giraffe*. What are some things you could say to someone who is acting like a Gloating Giraffe? ("I'm important, too." "Do you hear yourself?" "You're being snooty." "Do you think he/she is being snooty?") After a response is given, the round will be over. Then two new people will be chosen and we will repeat the activity.

Optional Activity:

Give each student a copy of the *Gloating Giraffe Story Picture* and crayons or markers. Allow the students to color the picture in class or to take it home to color. The pictures may be used as classroom posters.

GLOATING GIRAFFE STORY

Gloating Giraffe loved to stretch her long neck into the tops of the trees at the edge of the jungle. Since she was so much taller than anyone or anything else and could twist, turn, bend, and stretch her neck in so many ways, she was able to eat the best leaves. This gave her a feeling of power.

One day as she was eating delicious leaves only she could reach, she caught a glimpse of Neji and his two friends, Perty Parrot and Genka. Genka was called Skinny Dog Genka because he was a skinny, scruffy-looking dog. The three friends were playing near the edge of the jungle.

Gloating Giraffe immediately peered down over the trees so the three friends could see her. She glared at them in a very important way and spit out, "Who do you think you are? This is *my* jungle. Get out of here! You can't play here." Then she loped away with ease.

The three friends looked at each other in a surprised way and shrugged their shoulders. They felt a little bit afraid of the mean-sounding snooty giraffe, but they continued playing their game at the edge of the jungle. Little did they know that the self-important, snooty Gloating Giraffe would return.

And return she did. The giraffe came back to the edge of the jungle three more times. She stuck her long nose up into the air and ordered the three playmates to leave the jungle saying, "This is MY jungle, and you're not smart enough or important enough to join me in it."

Finally, Neji got tired of Gloating Giraffe's interruptions and tired of feeling unworthy to be in the jungle. He remembered what his mother had told him: "Always protect yourself."

Neji decided that he needed to protect his hurt feelings, so he said to the giraffe, "We're not leaving. It's a free jungle, and you are acting like a stuck-up bully. You think you're better than the rest of us and the owner of the jungle, but you're not."

Perty Parrot echoed, "Owner of the jungle. Owner of the jungle." Skinny Dog Genka agreed with a shrill, "Bark! Bark!"

Gloating Giraffe hadn't expected Neji and his friends to say anything to her. She could not believe what she was hearing. She was used to others thinking of her as the best and most important animal in the jungle. But these three, near the edge of her jungle, recognized her snootiness as bad manners. Gloating Giraffe's attitude had not worked on them.

So off Gloating Giraffe trotted, leaving Neji, Perty Parrot, and Skinny Dog Genka congratulating each other for sticking together.

MENACING MONKEY
GANGING UP ON OTHERS

Purpose:

To help students relate to a situation in which someone is ganged up on

Grade Levels: K-2

Materials Needed:

For The Leader:

☐ *Menacing Monkey Hat* (pages 232-236)
☐ *Menacing Monkey Story* (page 129)

For Each Student:

☐ Copy of the *Menacing Monkey Story Picture* (optional, page 192)
☐ Crayons or markers (optional)

Pre-Lesson Preparation:

If not constructed previously, make the *Menacing Monkey Hat* according to its directions.

Optional: Make a copy of the *Menacing Monkey Story Picture* for each student.

Lesson:

Introduce the lesson by asking:

What does the word *menacing* mean?" (It means to be a threat, danger, bully, etc.)

What does it mean to *gang up on* someone? (To pick on someone, to outnumber someone, etc.)

Today our story is about a menacing bully and his friends who do just that. They gang up on someone.

If you were all alone and a group started bothering you, how would you feel? (Bring out the feelings of fear, being overwhelmed, panic-stricken, etc.)

Before beginning the story, remind the students:

As I read our story, it is important for you to be a good listener. To do this, you must remember to use the parts of your body that help you to be a good listener. Who can tell me what body parts these are and what you should do with them? (Eyes should be facing the reader, hands should be still or in your lap, nose should be pointed toward the reader, mouth is closed, ears are hearing what the reader is saying, brain is thinking about what the reader is saying, and feet and legs are under your desk or crisscrossed.)

Read the *Menacing Monkey Story*.

Discussion Questions:

Ask the students the following questions:

1. **What part of the story do you remember best?** (This does not have to be in sequence, since the part shared is the part most meaningful to the student.)

2. **When the story was over, how did you feel? Why?**

3. **What did the monkeys do in the story that prove they are menacing?** (The monkeys ganged up on one person to annoy, scare, and hurt him.)

4. **Without using any names, have you ever seen people gang up on someone ? What happened?**

5. **What did the main character in the story do that was right? Wrong?**

6. **What did you learn from the story about how to handle a bully?**

Application:

Tell the students:

I will choose two people to come to the front of the room. One person will wear the *Menacing Monkey Hat*. The person wearing the hat has many friends and will say threatening things such as, "We're coming after you!" or "My friends and I will punch you out." Upon hearing a sentence like that, the other person will respond to the *monkey*. What are some things you could say to someone who is acting like a Menacing Monkey? (The other person might get help, leave quickly, or call loudly for help even if he or she is in a "keep quiet" place.) **After a response is given, the round will be over. Then two new people will be chosen and we will repeat the activity.**

Optional Activity:

Give each student a copy of the *Menacing Monkey Story Picture* and crayons or markers. Allow the students to color the picture in class or to take it home to color. The pictures may be used as classroom posters.

MENACING MONKEY STORY

Neji thought that monkeys were very popular and entertaining. Everyone always watched them. In fact, when monkeys were around, they generally got a lot of attention.

Neji approached a group of monkeys who were hanging and swinging in the trees over his head. He called to them and tried to get their attention. What he didn't realize was that the monkeys were also watching him. They saw that he was by himself, and they didn't want him around. Before Neji knew what was happening, the monkeys slowly descended from the trees and surrounded Neji. Even though Neji wanted to be friendly, the monkeys did not.

As the monkeys came closer and closer to Neji, he realized that this was not fun at all.

One monkey pulled Neji's hair. One pulled on his shirt while another monkey climbed up his leg. Neji wanted out of there and fast, but what could he do? He wished he had not come alone. Having a buddy with him would have been a better idea, but it was too late.

Neji tried to talk to the monkeys in a friendly way, but that definitely didn't work. Then he tried running away, but the monkeys were faster, and they were everywhere. Then he remembered what his mother told him: "Always protect yourself." That was something he should have done before he got into such a mess.

Neji stood his ground and yelled "STOP!" over and over. He yelled so loudly that others heard him and they ran toward Neji. When they saw the trouble he was in, they started to come to his rescue. The monkeys, seeing this, quickly left.

Neji thanked all those who came to his rescue. They made him promise to have a buddy with him next time he went into the jungle. Neji agreed and promised he would do that. This was a promise Neji knew he would keep.

129

HARASSING HIPPO
NAME-CALLING

Purpose:

To help students relate to a situation in which someone is calling names

Grade Levels: K-2

Materials Needed:

For The Leader:

- [ ] *Harassing Hippo Hat* (pages 237-240)
- [ ] *Harassing Hippo Story* (page 132)

For Each Student:

- [ ] Copy of the *Harassing Hippo Story Picture* (optional, page 193)
- [ ] Crayons or markers (optional)

Pre-Lesson Preparation:

If not constructed previously, make the *Harassing Hippo Hat* according to its directions.

Optional: Make a copy of the *Harassing Hippo Story Picture* for each student.

Lesson:

Introduce the lesson by saying:

> **Our story today is about name-calling. How do you feel if someone calls you names?** (Bring out the feelings of being hurt, ashamed, embarrassed, angry, etc.)

Before beginning the story, remind the students:

> **As I read our story, it is important for you to be a good listener. To do this, you must remember to use the parts of your body that help you to be a good listener. Who can tell me what body parts these are and what you should do with them?** (Eyes should be facing the reader, hands should be still or in your lap, nose

should be pointed toward the reader, mouth is closed, ears are hearing what the reader is saying, brain is thinking about what the reader is saying, and feet and legs are under your desk or crisscrossed.)

Read the *Harassing Hippo Story.*

Discussion Questions:

Ask the students the following questions:

1. **What part of the story do you remember best?** (This does not have to be in sequence, since the part shared is the part most meaningful to the student.)

2. **When the story was over, how did you feel? Why?**

3. **What does the hippopotamus do in the story to earn the title of *Harassing Hippo*?** (The hippo calls others names.)

4. **We cannot say an inappropriate name aloud, even though these names are sometimes used. If this is the type of name you have been called, just say "blank" for the name that you were called. Now, without saying the name of the person, has anyone ever called you names? What happened?**

5. **What did you learn from the story about how to handle a bully?**

Application:

Tell the students:

I will choose two people to come to the front of the room. One person will wear the *Harassing Hippo Hat*. In order not to hurt anyone's feelings, the person wearing the hat will say, "You're a blank." Upon hearing that sentence, the other person will respond to the *hippopotamus*. What are some things you could say to someone who is calling names? ("Don't treat me that way." "You're being a bully.") **After a response is given, the round will be over. Then two new people will be chosen and we will repeat the activity.**

Optional Activity:

Give each student a copy of the *Harassing Hippo Story Picture* and crayons or markers. Allow the students to color the picture in class or to take it home to color. The pictures may be used as classroom posters.

HARASSING HIPPO STORY

The three friends Neji, Perty Parrot, and Skinny Dog Genka enjoyed running, skipping, and jumping up and down through the jungle and by the river's edge. In fact, that's what they did almost every day. Whenever the three friends were nearby, Harassing Hippo spied on them. He hid under the deep water, with only his bulging eyes sticking out above his snout. Harassing Hippo wished that he could run and move as quickly as Neji, but he just couldn't. So, Harassing Hippo called Neji a name each time the boy came near the edge of the river.

The first time, Harassing Hippo called out, "Hi, Skippity Clippity" in a mocking voice as Neji skipped by, Neji just ignored Harassing Hippo's unfriendly words.

The next time, Harassing Hippo called out, "Hi, Funny Runny Bunny" as Neji ran past. Still Neji ignored Harassing Hippo's foolish ways. He did, however, feel angry at being called the crazy, mean name.

Then Harassing Hippo called out over and over again to Neji in a singsong fashion, "Neji Weji can't hop or pop." Neji tried to ignore Harassing Hippo again, but the anger was boiling inside of him. Then he began to remember what his mother had said: "Always protect yourself." And that's what he decided to do.

Neji stopped at the water's edge and answered the hiding hippo, "What did you say? That sounds like name-calling, and only bullies do that." Then Neji turned and left Harassing Hippo in the deep water.

Skinny Dog Genka barked a warning to Harassing Hippo. Perty Parrot swooped down with a warning flap of her wing at Harassing Hippo's big snout. Then Neji's two friends followed him to safety. With all of this going on, Harassing Hippo decided to dip under the water. He realized that he had just ruined a chance to make friends to play with. Now he was alone again.

REFUSING RHINO
DENIES EVERYTHING

Purpose:

To help students relate to a situation in which someone denies wrongdoing

Grade Levels: K-2

Materials Needed:

For The Leader:

☐ *Refusing Rhino Hat* (pages 241-244)
☐ *Refusing Rhino Story* (page 135)

For Each Student:

☐ Copy of the *Refusing Rhino Story Picture* (optional, page 194)
☐ Crayons or markers (optional)

Pre-Lesson Preparation:

If not constructed previously, make the *Refusing Rhino Hat* according to its directions.

Optional: Make a copy of the *Refusing Rhino Story Picture* for each student.

Lesson:

Introduce the lesson by saying:

> **Our story today is about a type of bully who denies or lies about ever doing anything wrong and sometimes even blames others for his or her own actions. How would you feel if you were around someone who always blamed others for things he or she actually did?** (Bring out the feelings of being nervous, unhappy, angry, etc.)

Before beginning the story, remind the students:

> **As I read our story, it is important for you to be a good listener. To do this, you must remember to use the parts of your body that help you to be a good lis-**

tener. **Who can tell me what body parts these are and what you should do with them?** (Eyes should be facing the reader, hands should be still or in your lap, nose should be pointed toward the reader, mouth is closed, ears are hearing what the reader is saying, brain is thinking about what the reader is saying, and feet and legs are under your desk or crisscrossed.)

Read the *Refusing Rhino Story.*

Discussion Questions:

Ask the students the following questions:

1. **What part of the story do you remember best?** (This does not have to be in sequence, since the part shared is the part most meaningful to the student.)

2. **When the story was over, how did you feel? Why?**

3. **What does the rhinoceros do in the story to earn the name Refusing Rhino?** (He refuses to admit what he has done. He lies.)

4. **Without using any names, have you ever heard a bully lying or denying doing anything wrong? What happened?**

5. **What did you learn from the story about how to handle a bully?**

Application:

Tell the students:

I will choose two people to come to the front of the room. One person will wear the *Refusing Rhino Hat.* The person wearing the hat will say, "It's not my fault. I didn't do it." Upon hearing those sentences, the other person will respond to the *rhinoceros.* What are some things that could be said to the denying, blaming Refusing Rhinoceros? ("That's lying to say you didn't do that." "I can't hear lies, so what did you say?" "Does anyone else think he/she is not telling the truth?") **After a response is given, the round will be over. Then two new people will be chosen and we will repeat the activity.**

Optional Activity:

Give each student a copy of the *Refusing Rhino Story Picture* and crayons or markers. Allow the students to color the picture in class or to take it home to color. The pictures may be used as classroom posters.

REFUSING RHINO STORY

Neji was busy building a tall tower with small pieces of wood. Higher and higher the tower went, shaking as each new piece of wood was placed on top of it. Perty Parrot sat quietly on her perch and watched. Skinny Dog Genka lay fast asleep by Neji's side.

Refusing Rhino peeked around a huge tree trunk Oh, how he would enjoy seeing that tall tower tumble to the ground with a clatter! He didn't think about how Neji would feel. Refusing Rhino just inched slowly out from behind the big tree trunk toward the growing tower. As quickly as a fly escaping from a fly swatter, Refusing Rhino ran past the tower, causing a sudden gust of air. The mighty tower toppled with a scattering noise as wood hit the ground. In seconds, the tower was totally demolished. Neji was shocked and angry to think Refusing Rhino would do such a mean thing.

Neji called out to Refusing Rhino, "You knocked down my tower on purpose! I spent a lot of time building it higher and higher. That was mean to knock it down."

Refusing Rhino stopped, turned around to face Neji, and called back, "I didn't do that. I didn't *touch* your tower. I was just running a race. I didn't even *see* your old tower." Neji knew that was a lie. After all, there was a lot of other ground that Refusing Rhino could have used. Then Neji remembered what his mother had said: "Always protect yourself."

So Neji again accused Refusing Rhino of knocking down his tower. In his firmest voice, he said, "You did that on purpose. You could have run way over there. Stay away unless you can play fair. You act like a bully."

Perty Parrot squawked, "Play fair. Play fair," and Skinny Dog Genka awoke from his nap and chased Refusing Rhino away.

The three friends taught Refusing Rhino a lesson. Now Refusing Rhino carefully watches what he does. He plays fairly with Neji and his friends because Refusing Rhino does not really want to act like a bully.

135

SNAPPY SNAKE
POOR MANNERS

Purpose:

To teach students to relate to a situation in which someone uses poor manners by whining and complaining

Grade Levels: K-2

Materials Needed:

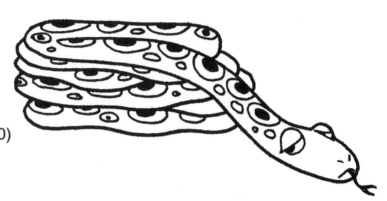

For The Leader:

☐ *Snappy Snake Hat* (pages 245-250)
☐ *Snappy Snake Story* (page 138)

For Each Student:

☐ Copy of the *Snappy Snake Story Picture* (optional, page 195)
☐ Crayons or markers (optional)

Pre-Lesson Preparation:

If not constructed previously, make the *Snappy Snake Hat* according to its directions.

Optional: Make a copy of the *Snappy Snake Story Picture* for each student.

Lesson:

Introduce the lesson by saying:

Our story today is about whining and complaining in order to get your own way. This type of behavior is bad manners. How do you think you would feel if someone you were with whined and complained about everything you were trying to do? (Bring out the feelings of being hurt, angry, disgusted, etc.)

Before beginning the story, remind the students:

As I read our story, it is important for you to be a good listener. To do this, you must remember to use the parts of your body that help you to be a good lis-

tener. **Who can tell me what body parts these are and what you should do with them?** (Eyes should be facing the reader, hands should be still or in your lap, nose should be pointed toward the reader, mouth is closed, ears are hearing what the reader is saying, brain is thinking about what the reader is saying, and feet and legs are under your desk or crisscrossed.)

Read the *Snappy Snake Story.*

Discussion Questions:

Ask the students the following questions:

1. **What part of the story do you remember best?** (This does not have to be in sequence, since the part shared is the part most meaningful to the student.)

2. **When the story was over, how did you feel? Why?**

3. **What does the snake do in the story to earn the name *Snappy Snake*?** (She snaps at the others over everything.)

4. **Without mentioning names, tell if you ever played with someone who was demanding and hard to please. What happened?**

5. **What did you learn from the story about how to handle a bully?**

Application:

Tell the students:

I will choose two people to come to the front of the room. One person will wear the *Snappy Snake Hat*. The person with the hat will whine, "I don't like this. Can't we do something else?" Upon hearing that question, the other person will respond to the *snake*. What are some things you could say to someone who whines and has bad manners? ("I can't play with you if you keep whining." "Stop whining." "Go play with someone else if you aren't happy here.") **After a response is given, the round will be over. Then two new people will be chosen and we will repeat the activity.**

Optional Activity:

Give each student a copy of the *Snappy Snake Story Picture* and crayons or markers. Allow the students to color the picture in class or to take it home to color. The pictures may be used as classroom posters.

SNAPPY SNAKE STORY

Neji and his two friends, Perty Parrot and Skinny Dog Genka, had a full picnic basket under their favorite shade tree. They spread out the red- and white-cloth and began unloading the terrific lunch that Neji's mother had packed for them. They had invited Snappy Snake to come along, thinking that would make this an extra-special fun time for everyone.

Snappy Snake lived in the jungle next to Neji's house and played with the three friends when Neji's mother gave them permission. They needed permission to play with Snappy because arguments and fussing would sometimes start up and Neji's mother would say, "That's very bad manners to argue and fuss like that. Separate and cool off." The four of them did not always get along.

Snappy Snake was known to be whiney and hard to please. She would start by disagreeing with everything, then complain about things that she didn't like. Sometimes she was no fun at all. To quiet her down, Neji would often give in to Snappy Snake's demands.

Today was no exception. Snappy Snake began by saying, "I hate this sandwich. YUCK! It's gross. I want something else. I want something else." Then she threw the food down on the ground and squeezed it into a mashed-up ball. Next, she whined that she didn't have enough cookies, and she made everyone else give her theirs.

No matter how the others tried to make Snappy Snake happy, she just wasn't satisfied. She kept picking out faults with the food and making the picnic unpleasant. It was so bad that the three friends got tummy aches from all of the complaining that they had to listen to from Snappy Snake. Her whining gave them all headaches.

Finally, enough was enough. Neji, Perty Parrot, and Skinny Dog Genka got up, gathered all the goodies that they had looked forward to enjoying, and moved to another shade tree. Snappy Snake stayed where she was, curled up in a frightful position. As they left, Neji said, "We need to separate and cool off, just like my mom usually tells us to do. Go home, Snappy Snake, and leave us alone." Perty Parrot agreed as she squawked, "Go home! Go home!" Skinny Dog Genka barked to show that he agreed. Snappy Snake hissed in surprise.

Snappy Snake slithered away in disappointment. Always before, Neji had just kept trying to please her. Now she had no one to be with. Snappy Snake hadn't expected to be stopped before she actually got started. Now she was all alone, and she still wanted to play. But Snappy Snake knew, down deep in her curvy body, that this was the end to today's fun.

CROAKING CROCODILE
YELLING

Purpose:

To teach students to relate to a situation in which someone yells at them

Grade Levels: K-2

Materials Needed:

For The Leader:

☐ *Croaking Crocodile Hat* (pages 251-255)
☐ *Croaking Crocodile Story* (page 141)

For Each Student:

☐ Copy of the *Croaking Crocodile Story Picture* (optional, page 196)
☐ Crayons or markers (optional)

Pre-Lesson Preparation:

If not constructed previously, make the *Croaking Crocodile Hat* according to its directions.

Optional: Make a copy of the *Croaking Crocodile Story Picture* for each student.

Lesson:

Introduce the lesson by saying:

Our story today is about a bully who yells a lot. How do you think you would feel if someone yelled at you a lot? (Bring out the idea of feeling hurt, discouraged, sad, stupid, etc.)

Before beginning the story, remind the students:

As I read our story, it is important for you to be a good listener. To do this, you must remember to use the parts of your body that help you to be a good lis-

tener. **Who can tell me what body parts these are and what you should do with them?** (Eyes should be facing the reader, hands should be still or in your lap, nose should be pointed toward the reader, mouth is closed, ears are hearing what the reader is saying, brain is thinking about what the reader is saying, and feet and legs are under your desk or crisscrossed.)

Read the *Croaking Crocodile Story.*

Discussion Questions:

Ask the students the following questions:

1. **What part of the story do you remember best?** (This does not have to be in sequence, since the part shared is the part most meaningful to the student.)

2. **When the story was over, how did you feel? Why?**

3. **Why do you think the crocodile is called** *Croaking Crocodile***?** (The sounds she makes are croaks and the crocodile yells at others.)

4. **Without mentioning names, tell if any of your friends ever yelled at you a lot. What happened?**

5. **What did you learn from the story about how to handle a bully?**

Application:

Tell the students:

I will choose two people to come to the front of the room. One person will wear the *Croaking Crocodile Hat***. The person with the hat will yell, "Get away." Upon hearing that sentence, the other person will respond to the** *crocodile.* **What are some things you could say to someone who is yelling at you?** ("I'll leave you alone until you can calm down." "Stop yelling at me." "Don't treat me that way.") **After a response is given, the round will be over. Then two new people will be chosen and we will repeat the activity.**

Optional Activity:

Give each student a copy of the *Croaking Crocodile Story Picture* and crayons or markers. Allow the students to color the picture in class or to take it home to color. The pictures may be used as classroom posters.

140

CROAKING CROCODILE STORY

Neji, Perty Parrot, and Skinny Dog Genka threw stones into the river to splash in the water. Perty Parrot, of course, picked up stones in her beak and then flew over the water to drop them with a *kerplunk.* Skinny Dog Genka, of course, scraped up a stone by digging quickly with his paws. His back was toward the river, so the stones flew out into the water in an uncontrolled direction going *plop, plop, plop.* But Neji picked up flat stones to skip across the water. Some of Neji's stones skipped three times before sinking to the bottom of the river.

The three friends were having fun. They didn't realize that a grumpy crocodile floating nearby was trying to get some sleep

"Croak! Croak!" the big crocodile croaked loudly. "Get out! Get out!"

The three friends turned and began to leave the crabby crocodile's territory in a hurry. Her croaking was so loud it hurt their ears. Shaking with fear, they hid in the safety of the trees.

Then Neji remembered what his mother had said: "Always protect yourself." Neji turned and walked calmly back to the river. In his nicest voice, he said, "Yelling hurts my ears." Then, Perty Parrot repeated in her nicest squawk, "Yelling hurts my ears. Yelling hurts my ears." Skinny Dog Genka added his remarks by panting happily in view of the crabby crocodile.

The crocodile watched the three friends as they stuck together, helping one another. She smiled her ferocious smile and swam away to find a log on which to nap, far away from the three noisy friends. It didn't take her long, and it wasn't much trouble. After all, she didn't want to use up too much energy, croaking her loud croc croak again and again. There she rested on her new log, watching the three and waiting to catch one of them alone.

141

REPRODUCIBLE
ACTIVITY
PAGES

BULLY WORLD CATEGORIES

Physical size

Color of hair

Grades

Clothing

Mothers

Skin color

Sports ability

Artistic ability

Musical ability

Computer ability

Eyesight

Noses

Ears

Countries

Houses

Classroom Behavior

You play an instrument
in the school band better
than the bully.

CONQUERING BULLIES: BULLY WORLD CARDS
© 2005 MAR*CO PRODUCTS, INC. 1-800-448-2197

You are shorter than the bully.

CONQUERING BULLIES: BULLY WORLD CARDS
© 2005 MAR*CO PRODUCTS, INC. 1-800-448-2197

Your hair is a different color
than the bully's hair.

CONQUERING BULLIES: BULLY WORLD CARDS
© 2005 MAR*CO PRODUCTS, INC. 1-800-448-2197

You get better grades
than the bully.

CONQUERING BULLIES: BULLY WORLD CARDS
© 2005 MAR*CO PRODUCTS, INC. 1-800-448-2197

You are taller than the bully.

CONQUERING BULLIES: BULLY WORLD CARDS
© 2005 MAR*CO PRODUCTS, INC. 1-800-448-2197

You get poorer grades
than the bully.

CONQUERING BULLIES: BULLY WORLD CARDS
© 2005 MAR*CO PRODUCTS, INC. 1-800-448-2197

Your mom works at a job outside
the home, and the bully's mom
does not.

CONQUERING BULLIES: BULLY WORLD CARDS
© 2005 MAR*CO PRODUCTS, INC. 1-800-448-2197

You skin is a different color
than the bully's skin.

CONQUERING BULLIES: BULLY WORLD CARDS
© 2005 MAR*CO PRODUCTS, INC. 1-800-448-2197

You are better in sports
than the bully.

CONQUERING BULLIES: BULLY WORLD CARDS
© 2005 MAR*CO PRODUCTS, INC. 1-800-448-2197

You are not as good in
sports as the bully.

CONQUERING BULLIES: BULLY WORLD CARDS
© 2005 MAR*CO PRODUCTS, INC. 1-800-448-2197

You are better in art than the bully.

CONQUERING BULLIES: BULLY WORLD CARDS
© 2005 MAR*CO PRODUCTS, INC. 1-800-448-2197

You are not as good in
art as the bully.

CONQUERING BULLIES: BULLY WORLD CARDS
© 2005 MAR*CO PRODUCTS, INC. 1-800-448-2197

The bully plays in the school band, and you do not.

You are a computer whiz, and the bully is not.

You wear glasses and the bully does not.

The bully wears glasses and you do not.

Your nose is much larger than the bully's nose.

The bully has much larger ears than you.

You come from a different country than the bully.

The bully wears different types of clothing than you wear.

You live in an apartment and the bully lives in a house.

You and the bully are both good in art.

You sit quietly in class, and the bully interrupts when other kids are talking.

You and the bully have the same color hair.

You and the bully have
the same color skin.

CONQUERING BULLIES: BULLY WORLD CARDS
© 2005 MAR*CO PRODUCTS, INC. 1-800-448-2197

You and the bully make
the same grades in math.

CONQUERING BULLIES: BULLY WORLD CARDS
© 2005 MAR*CO PRODUCTS, INC. 1-800-448-2197

You and the bully come
from the same country.

CONQUERING BULLIES: BULLY WORLD CARDS
© 2005 MAR*CO PRODUCTS, INC. 1-800-448-2197

Neither you nor the
bully wears glasses.

CONQUERING BULLIES: BULLY WORLD CARDS
© 2005 MAR*CO PRODUCTS, INC. 1-800-448-2197

You and the bully dress alike.

CONQUERING BULLIES: BULLY WORLD CARDS
© 2005 MAR*CO PRODUCTS, INC. 1-800-448-2197

Both you and the bully
live in houses.

CONQUERING BULLIES: BULLY WORLD CARDS
© 2005 MAR*CO PRODUCTS, INC. 1-800-448-2197

You and the bully are
the same height.

CONQUERING BULLIES: BULLY WORLD CARDS
© 2005 MAR*CO PRODUCTS, INC. 1-800-448-2197

Your mom and the bully's mom
work in the same office.

CONQUERING BULLIES: BULLY WORLD CARDS
© 2005 MAR*CO PRODUCTS, INC. 1-800-448-2197

You and the bully are
both on the soccer team.

CONQUERING BULLIES: BULLY WORLD CARDS
© 2005 MAR*CO PRODUCTS, INC. 1-800-448-2197

You always do your homework.
The bully makes others do
his/her homework.

CONQUERING BULLIES: BULLY WORLD CARDS
© 2005 MAR*CO PRODUCTS, INC. 1-800-448-2197

You ask a classmate when you
need something. The bully takes
what he/she wants without asking.

CONQUERING BULLIES: BULLY WORLD CARDS
© 2005 MAR*CO PRODUCTS, INC. 1-800-448-2197

You and the bully both play
an instrument in the school band.

CONQUERING BULLIES: BULLY WORLD CARDS
© 2005 MAR*CO PRODUCTS, INC. 1-800-448-2197

OLD MACDONALD HAD A SCHOOL
Sung to the tune of
Old MacDonald Had a Farm

Old MacDonald had a school,
E-I-E-I-O.
And in that school there was a bully,
E-I-E-I-O.
With a growl, growl here,
And a growl, growl there.
Here a growl, there a growl,
Everywhere a growl, growl.
Old MacDonald had a school,
E-I-E-I-O.

Old MacDonald saw Hurtful Hyena,
E-I-E-I-O.
With a "You can't play," here,
And a "You can't play" there.
Here a "You can't play,"
There a "You can't play,"
Everywhere a "You can't play."
Old MacDonald had a school,
E-I-E-I-O.

Old MacDonald saw Refusing Rhino,
E-I-E-I-O,
With an "I didn't do it" here,
And an "I didn't do it" there.
Here an "I didn't do it,
There an "I didn't do it,
Everywhere an "I didn't do it."
Old MacDonald had a school,
E-I-E-I-O.

Old MacDonald saw Harassing Hippo,
E-I-E-I-O.
With a name-calling here,
And a name-calling there.
Here a name-calling,
There a name-calling,
Everywhere a name-calling.
Old MacDonald had a school,
E-I-E-I-O.

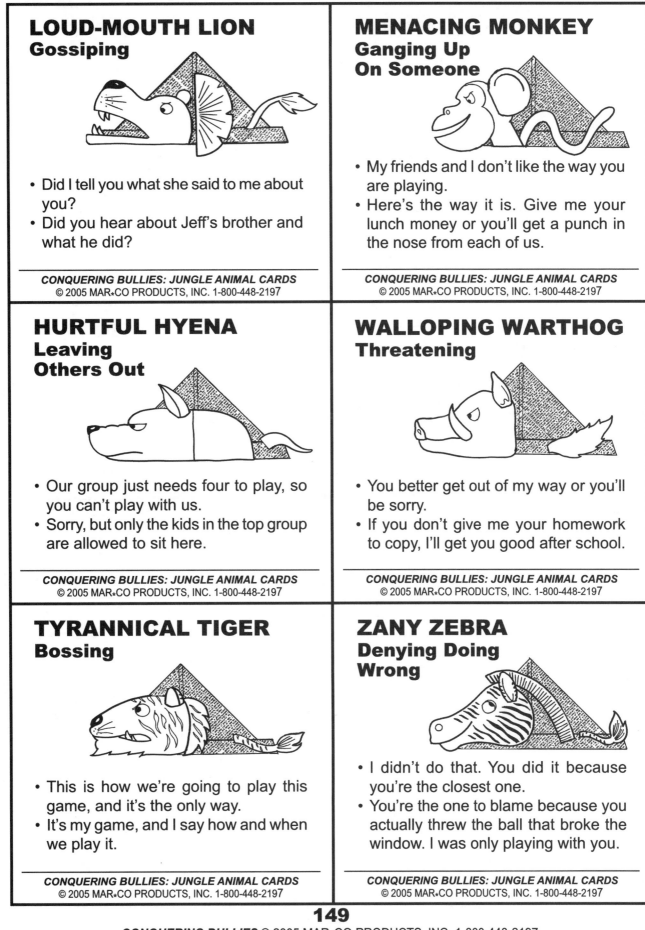

LOUD-MOUTH LION
Gossiping

- Did I tell you what she said to me about you?
- Did you hear about Jeff's brother and what he did?

CONQUERING BULLIES: JUNGLE ANIMAL CARDS
© 2005 MAR*CO PRODUCTS, INC. 1-800-448-2197

MENACING MONKEY
Ganging Up On Someone

- My friends and I don't like the way you are playing.
- Here's the way it is. Give me your lunch money or you'll get a punch in the nose from each of us.

CONQUERING BULLIES: JUNGLE ANIMAL CARDS
© 2005 MAR*CO PRODUCTS, INC. 1-800-448-2197

HURTFUL HYENA
Leaving Others Out

- Our group just needs four to play, so you can't play with us.
- Sorry, but only the kids in the top group are allowed to sit here.

CONQUERING BULLIES: JUNGLE ANIMAL CARDS
© 2005 MAR*CO PRODUCTS, INC. 1-800-448-2197

WALLOPING WARTHOG
Threatening

- You better get out of my way or you'll be sorry.
- If you don't give me your homework to copy, I'll get you good after school.

CONQUERING BULLIES: JUNGLE ANIMAL CARDS
© 2005 MAR*CO PRODUCTS, INC. 1-800-448-2197

TYRANNICAL TIGER
Bossing

- This is how we're going to play this game, and it's the only way.
- It's my game, and I say how and when we play it.

CONQUERING BULLIES: JUNGLE ANIMAL CARDS
© 2005 MAR*CO PRODUCTS, INC. 1-800-448-2197

ZANY ZEBRA
Denying Doing Wrong

- I didn't do that. You did it because you're the closest one.
- You're the one to blame because you actually threw the ball that broke the window. I was only playing with you.

CONQUERING BULLIES: JUNGLE ANIMAL CARDS
© 2005 MAR*CO PRODUCTS, INC. 1-800-448-2197

ERUPTING ELEPHANT
**Giving
Put-downs**

- You're too little to play with us.
- What a lousy shot! No wonder we lost the game.

CONQUERING BULLIES: JUNGLE ANIMAL CARDS
© 2005 MAR∗CO PRODUCTS, INC. 1-800-448-2197

GLOATING GIRAFFE
Snooty

- I *always* get picked first! Everyone likes me.
- You take the bus to school? My parents always drive me.

CONQUERING BULLIES: JUNGLE ANIMAL CARDS
© 2005 MAR∗CO PRODUCTS, INC. 1-800-448-2197

HARASSING HIPPO
Name-Calling

- You're such a nerd!
- You're such a wimp!

CONQUERING BULLIES: JUNGLE ANIMAL CARDS
© 2005 MAR∗CO PRODUCTS, INC. 1-800-448-2197

REFUSING RHINO
Lying

- I always get an "A" in every subject.
- I never get sick.

CONQUERING BULLIES: JUNGLE ANIMAL CARDS
© 2005 MAR∗CO PRODUCTS, INC. 1-800-448-2197

SNAPPY SNAKE
Being Rude

- Get out of my way! I want to be first in line.
- So what if it's the last cookie? I'm hungry and I want it, now!

CONQUERING BULLIES: JUNGLE ANIMAL CARDS
© 2005 MAR∗CO PRODUCTS, INC. 1-800-448-2197

CROAKING CROCODILE
Yelling

- It's my turn! Get away!
- Quiet! Nobody wants to listen to you.

CONQUERING BULLIES: JUNGLE ANIMAL CARDS
© 2005 MAR∗CO PRODUCTS, INC. 1-800-448-2197

THE BULLY IN THE SCHOOL
Sung to the tune of
The Farmer In The Dell

The bully in the school,
The bully in the school,
Hi ho the dario,
The bully in the school.

The bully picks a fight,
The bully picks a fight,
Hi ho the dario,
The bully picks a fight.

The bully calls a name,
The bully calls a name,
Hi ho the dario,
The bully calls a name.

The bully yells and screams,
The bully yells and screams,
Hi ho the dario,
The bully yells and screams.

The bully doesn't share,
The bully doesn't share,
Hi ho the dario,
The bully doesn't share.

The bully leaves you out,
The bully leaves you out,
Hi ho the dario,
The bully leaves you out.

The bully puts you down,
The bully puts you down,
Hi ho the dario,
The bully puts you down.

The bully gangs up on you,
The bully gangs up on you,
Hi ho the dario,
The bully gangs up on you.

The bully does no wrong,
The bully does no wrong,
Hi ho the dario,
The bully does no wrong.

SPOT THE BULLY SITUATION LIST

Read each situation aloud.

🗩 **SITUATION 1:** Carrie comes onto the playground and approaches a small group of her classmates. She says, "Let's play a game together." The girls answer her by saying, "_____ ."
Type of Bullying Response: Put-downs
Possible Bullying Responses:
"You're too stupid to play."
 "No way, Fumblefingers! You always drop the ball."

🗩 **SITUATION 2:** Tran has recently come from another country. He doesn't know the language well. When he tries to ask a group of boys a question, one of them replies, "_____ ."
Type of Bullying Response: Name-calling
Possible Bullying Response:
"Hey, Mumble Mouth! Nobody can understand you."
"Mush Mouth! Don't you know how to talk?"

🗩 **SITUATION 3:** In the middle of a soccer game, Luke acts like a bully when he notices Rick is not playing the game the way Luke believes he should. Luke says, "_____ ."
Type of Bullying Response: Yelling
Possible Bullying Responses:
"Stop! You don't know what you're doing."
 "You're not playing the right way."

🗩 **SITUATION 4:** In social studies, Linda and two other classmates are assigned a project to do together. Linda knows exactly what she wants the others to do and says, "_____ ."
Type of Bullying Response: Bossiness
Possible Bullying Responses:
"If we're smart, we'll do it my way.
 "I know exactly how to do this project. First, I will assign each of you a part. When you are finished, you can bring it to me for me to okay."

🗩 **SITUATION 5:** Molly and Megan are playing a game during indoor recess. Megan sees Kyla coming toward them and says, "_____ ."
Type of Bullying Response: Gossiping
Possible Bullying Response:
"Look out, here comes Kyla! We can't play with her! Her father is in jail."
"It's Kyla! Did you know her brother was caught shoplifting?"

SITUATION 6: Juan has been waiting in line at the water fountain. When his turn is next, Lionel pushes in front of him, saying, "_____."
Type of Bullying Response: Threatening
Possible Bullying Responses:
"Get out of my way, Slowpoke."
"Let me in front of you or after school you'll be sorry."

SITUATION 7: Greta is having a birthday party and has invited every girl in her class except June. When asked why she didn't include June, she said, "_____."
Type of Bullying Response: Leaving a person out
Possible Bullying Response:
"She would never fit in with the rest of us."
"June's family doesn't have much money. She probably can't afford anything I would want, anyway."

SITUATION 8: When Clark sees Becky take his coat off the coat rack, throw it on the floor, and put hers there instead, he asks, "Hey, why did you throw my coat on the floor?" Becky isn't going to admit she did it. She says, "_____."
Type of Bullying Response: Denial
Possible Bullying Responses:
"I didn't do that. It just fell off by itself."
"Don't blame me for things you do yourself."

SITUATION 9: Billy has signed up to use the computer from 10:00 to 10:30. When he goes to the computer station at 10 o'clock, Patty is still working on the computer. She says, "_____."
Type of Bullying Response: Rudeness
Possible Bullying Response:
"I don't care if it is your time to use the computer. I am not giving it up!"
"I was here first, and I am not leaving."

SITUATION 10: Margo is really excited about her new sweater. When she shows it to Leona, Leona says, "_____."
Type of Bullying Response: Snooty
Possible Bullying Response:
"Cute sweater. But why did you buy last year's style?"
"That's new? I saw it on the sale table the other day when I bought one from the table with the new fashions."

CONQUERING BULLIES © 2005 MAR✱CO PRODUCTS, INC. 1-800-448-2197

SITUATION 1:

Type of Bullying Response:

Put-down

Respond by saying (choose one):

"You're too stupid to play."

"No way, Fumblefingers!
You always drop the ball."

SITUATION 2:

Type of Bullying Response:

Name-calling

Respond by saying (choose one):

"Hey, Mumble Mouth!
Nobody can understand you."

"Mush Mouth! Don't you
know how to talk?"

SITUATION 3:

Type of Bullying Response:

Yelling

Respond by saying (choose one):

"Stop! You don't know what you're doing."

"You're not playing the right way."

SITUATION 4:

Type of Bullying Response:

Bossiness

Respond by saying (choose one):

"If we're smart, we'll do it my way."

"I know exactly how to do this project.
First, I will assign each of you a part.
When you are finished, you can bring it
to me for me to okay."

SITUATION 5:

Type of Bullying Response:

Gossiping

Respond by saying (choose one):

"Look out, here comes Kyla! We can't
play with her! Her father is in jail."

"It's Kyla! Did you know her brother
was caught shoplifting?"

SITUATION 6:

Type of Bullying Response:

Threatening

Respond by saying (choose one):

"Get out of my way, Slowpoke."

"Let me in front of you or after
school you'll be sorry."

SITUATION 7:

Type of Bullying Response:

Leaving a person out

Respond by saying (choose one):

She would never fit in with the rest of us."

"June's family doesn't have much money. She probably can't afford anything I would want, anyway."

SITUATION 8:

Type of Bullying Response:

Denial

Respond by saying (choose one):

"I didn't do that. It just fell off by itself."

"Don't blame me for things you do yourself."

SITUATION 9:

Type of Bullying Response:

Rudeness

Respond by saying (choose one):

"I don't care if it is your time to use the computer. I am not giving it up!"

"I was here first, and I am not leaving."

SITUATION 10:

Type of Bullying Response:

Snooty

Respond by saying (choose one):

"Cute sweater. But why did you buy last year's style?"

"That's new? I saw it on the sale table the other day when I bought one from the table with the new fashions."

YOU ARE NOT A BULLY!

YOU ARE NOT A BULLY!

BULLY BOPPER LIST

Directions: Below are a list of *Negative Talk* statements and a list of *Positive Talk* statements. Read each one aloud. Do not read them as they are listed. Mix them up, going from one category to another.

Negative Talk:

You're stupid, and I don't associate with stupid people. (Gloating Giraffe)

You're a scaredy cat. (Harrassing Hippo)

We're playing what I want to play! (Tyrannical Tiger)

Give it to me now or I'm going to hit you. (Walloping Warthog)

It wasn't my fault. Get over it, NOW! (Refusing Rhino)

This is the worst time I have ever had. (Snappy Snake)

You can't be on our team. (Hurtful Hyena)

You'll never be good at anything. (Erupting Elephant)

Don't say anything, but I heard her father lost his job. (Loud-Mouth Lion)

Positive Talk:

You're my friend.

You're "cool."

I like talking with you.

You're good at that.

Are you hurt?

We'll talk about it.

You're fun to play with.

I know you can do it.

You're smart.

You can bring your grades up.

IF BULLY
Sung to the tune of
If You're Happy And You Know It

If Bully yells at you, hands on ears.
(PUT HANDS OVER EARS.)
If Bully yells at you, hands on ears.
(PUT HANDS OVER EARS.)
If Bully yells at you, find something else to do.
If Bully yells at you, hands on ears.
(PUT HANDS OVER EARS.)

If Bully leaves you out, find a friend.
(PUT HAND OVER TOP OF EYES, AS IF LOOKING.)
If Bully leaves you out, find a friend.
(PUT HAND OVER TOP OF EYES, AS IF LOOKING.)
If Bully leaves you out, don't cry and yell out.
If Bully leaves you out, find a friend.
(PUT HAND OVER TOP OF EYES, AS IF LOOKING.)

If Bully calls a name, shake your finger.
(SHAKE YOUR FINGER, "NO.")
If Bully calls a name, shake your finger.
(SHAKE YOUR FINGER, "NO.")
If Bully calls a name, go and find another game.
If Bully calls a name, shake your finger.
(SHAKE YOUR FINGER, "NO.")

If Bully threatens you, tell your mom.
(PUT HANDS AROUND MOUTH, AS IF CALLING.)
If Bully threatens you, tell your dad.
(PUT HANDS AROUND MOUTH, AS IF CALLING.)
If Bully threatens you, get some help for you, too.
If Bully threatens you, tell your mom.
(PUT HANDS AROUND MOUTH, AS IF CALLING.)

If Bully has bad manners, make a frown.
(PUT FINGERS ON EACH CORNER OF THE MOUTH AND PULL YOUR FINGERS DOWN INTO A FROWN.)
If Bully has bad manners, make a frown.
(PUT FINGERS ON EACH CORNER OF THE MOUTH AND PULL YOUR FINGERS DOWN INTO A FROWN.)
If Bully has bad manners, just keep your good manners.
If Bully has bad manners, make a frown.
(PUT FINGERS ON EACH CORNER OF THE MOUTH AND PULL YOUR FINGERS DOWN INTO A FROWN.)

HOT/COLD STATEMENTS

Directions: Select a statement from the list below each time the group of three students needs to change direction. Vary your selection of statements from "hot" to "cold."

Hot Statements (What a person who is not a bully might say)

Can you come over to my house to play on Saturday?

Go ahead, you were here first.

Great new shoes!

Let me help you.

Let's eat lunch together.

How did you get hurt?

I'll go with you to get help.

I'm going to the library. I'll take your book back for you.

Will you be my partner on the social studies project?

Let's play checkers at recess.

Cold Statements (What a bully might say)

Get away from us! Nobody here wants you around.

You're a wimp.

If you get in my way, I'll hit you.

Crybaby! Crybaby! Gonna run home to your mama?

You're ugly.

You can't be on our team. You can't even catch a ball.

Go to the end of the line. Nobody wants to drink water after you've touched the fountain.

Be your friend? You must be kidding!

You didn't hear what I said? With ears as big as yours, I thought you could hear anything anywhere.

Where did you get those shoes? At the horseshoe factory?

OSTRICH HEAD CARD

I'VE BEEN WORKING WITH A BULLY
Sung to the tune of
I've Been Working On The Railroad

I've been working with a bully,
Every day in class.
I've been working with a bully,
And I tell myself, "Alas."
Don't you hear the bully shouting?
Can't you tell that he is mean?
I'll tell the teacher quickly,
Bully go away.
Bully go away, bully go away, bully go away from me-e-e.
Bully go away, bully go away, bully go away from me.

I've been working with a bully,
Every day in class.
I've been working with a bully,
And I tell myself, "Alas."
Don't you hear the bully shouting?
Can't you tell that she is mean?
I'll tell the teacher quickly,
Bully go away.
Bully go away, bully go away, bully go away from me-e-e.
Bully go away, bully go away, bully go away from me.

BREAKS THE CODE OF SILENCE

Stop that!

CONQUERING BULLIES: CODE OF SILENCE CARDS
© 2005 MAR∗CO PRODUCTS, INC. 1-800-448-2197

BREAKS THE CODE OF SILENCE

Don't treat me that way.

CONQUERING BULLIES: CODE OF SILENCE CARDS
© 2005 MAR∗CO PRODUCTS, INC. 1-800-448-2197

BREAKS THE CODE OF SILENCE

Don't treat my friend that way.

CONQUERING BULLIES: CODE OF SILENCE CARDS
© 2005 MAR∗CO PRODUCTS, INC. 1-800-448-2197

BREAKS THE CODE OF SILENCE

I'm going to get the teacher.

CONQUERING BULLIES: CODE OF SILENCE CARDS
© 2005 MAR∗CO PRODUCTS, INC. 1-800-448-2197

BREAKS THE CODE OF SILENCE

My parents will be angry about this.

CONQUERING BULLIES: CODE OF SILENCE CARDS
© 2005 MAR∗CO PRODUCTS, INC. 1-800-448-2197

BREAKS THE CODE OF SILENCE

I can't play with you if you act that way.

CONQUERING BULLIES: CODE OF SILENCE CARDS
© 2005 MAR∗CO PRODUCTS, INC. 1-800-448-2197

BREAKS THE CODE OF SILENCE

I'll stay away from you until you can act OK.

CONQUERING BULLIES: CODE OF SILENCE CARDS
© 2005 MAR∗CO PRODUCTS, INC. 1-800-448-2197

BREAKS THE CODE OF SILENCE

Don't do that any more.

CONQUERING BULLIES: CODE OF SILENCE CARDS
© 2005 MAR∗CO PRODUCTS, INC. 1-800-448-2197

BREAKS THE CODE OF SILENCE

I'm going to keep my eye on you.

CONQUERING BULLIES: CODE OF SILENCE CARDS
© 2005 MAR∗CO PRODUCTS, INC. 1-800-448-2197

BREAKS THE CODE OF SILENCE

Leave me alone.

CONQUERING BULLIES: CODE OF SILENCE CARDS
© 2005 MAR∗CO PRODUCTS, INC. 1-800-448-2197

BREAKS THE CODE OF SILENCE

You're being a bully.

CONQUERING BULLIES: CODE OF SILENCE CARDS
© 2005 MAR∗CO PRODUCTS, INC. 1-800-448-2197

BREAKS THE CODE OF SILENCE

That's mean.

CONQUERING BULLIES: CODE OF SILENCE CARDS
© 2005 MAR∗CO PRODUCTS, INC. 1-800-448-2197

BREAKS THE CODE OF SILENCE

What makes you want
to act this way?

CONQUERING BULLIES: CODE OF SILENCE CARDS
© 2005 MAR∗CO PRODUCTS, INC. 1-800-448-2197

DOESN'T BREAK THE CODE OF SILENCE

I'm a rat if I tell.

CONQUERING BULLIES: CODE OF SILENCE CARDS
© 2005 MAR∗CO PRODUCTS, INC. 1-800-448-2197

DOESN'T BREAK THE CODE OF SILENCE

It only happens once in a while.

CONQUERING BULLIES: CODE OF SILENCE CARDS
© 2005 MAR∗CO PRODUCTS, INC. 1-800-448-2197

DOESN'T BREAK THE CODE OF SILENCE

It's useless to speak up.

CONQUERING BULLIES: CODE OF SILENCE CARDS
© 2005 MAR∗CO PRODUCTS, INC. 1-800-448-2197

DOESN'T BREAK THE CODE OF SILENCE

Nobody can help
me, anyway.

CONQUERING BULLIES: CODE OF SILENCE CARDS
© 2005 MAR∗CO PRODUCTS, INC. 1-800-448-2197

DOESN'T BREAK THE CODE OF SILENCE

Maybe I misunderstood
what was said.

CONQUERING BULLIES: CODE OF SILENCE CARDS
© 2005 MAR∗CO PRODUCTS, INC. 1-800-448-2197

DOESN'T BREAK THE CODE OF SILENCE

Maybe he/she didn't
mean to do that.

CONQUERING BULLIES: CODE OF SILENCE CARDS
© 2005 MAR∗CO PRODUCTS, INC. 1-800-448-2197

DOESN'T BREAK THE CODE OF SILENCE

You deserve to be hurt.

CONQUERING BULLIES: CODE OF SILENCE CARDS
© 2005 MAR∗CO PRODUCTS, INC. 1-800-448-2197

DOESN'T BREAK THE CODE OF SILENCE

No one will believe you.

CONQUERING BULLIES: CODE OF SILENCE CARDS
© 2005 MAR∗CO PRODUCTS, INC. 1-800-448-2197

DOESN'T BREAK THE CODE OF SILENCE

Maybe he will go away.

CONQUERING BULLIES: CODE OF SILENCE CARDS
© 2005 MAR∗CO PRODUCTS, INC. 1-800-448-2197

DOESN'T BREAK THE CODE OF SILENCE

What can I do about it?

CONQUERING BULLIES: CODE OF SILENCE CARDS
© 2005 MAR∗CO PRODUCTS, INC. 1-800-448-2197

DOESN'T BREAK THE CODE OF SILENCE

Oh, well, no one will
listen to me, anyway.

CONQUERING BULLIES: CODE OF SILENCE CARDS
© 2005 MAR∗CO PRODUCTS, INC. 1-800-448-2197

DOESN'T BREAK THE CODE OF SILENCE

Everyone always picks
on me, anyway.

CONQUERING BULLIES: CODE OF SILENCE CARDS
© 2005 MAR∗CO PRODUCTS, INC. 1-800-448-2197

DOESN'T BREAK THE CODE OF SILENCE

If I say anything,
no one will ever like me.

CONQUERING BULLIES: CODE OF SILENCE CARDS
© 2005 MAR∗CO PRODUCTS, INC. 1-800-448-2197

DOESN'T BREAK THE CODE OF SILENCE

I can stand it. Pretty soon
they'll find someone else
to pick on.

CONQUERING BULLIES: CODE OF SILENCE CARDS
© 2005 MAR∗CO PRODUCTS, INC. 1-800-448-2197

DOESN'T BREAK THE CODE OF SILENCE

It's not worth getting
beat up about.

CONQUERING BULLIES: CODE OF SILENCE CARDS
© 2005 MAR∗CO PRODUCTS, INC. 1-800-448-2197

DOESN'T BREAK THE CODE OF SILENCE

I don't want anyone to know
how bad they make me feel.

CONQUERING BULLIES: CODE OF SILENCE CARDS
© 2005 MAR∗CO PRODUCTS, INC. 1-800-448-2197

DOESN'T BREAK THE CODE OF SILENCE

Keep my mouth shut. Take it.
And go on with my life.

CONQUERING BULLIES: CODE OF SILENCE CARDS
© 2005 MAR∗CO PRODUCTS, INC. 1-800-448-2197

Situation 1:
Everyone is lined up
at the fountain to get
a drink of water.

Situation 2:
The group is outside
playing a ball game.

Situation 3:
Everyone is in the
library doing research
on the same subject.

Situation 4:
The group is trying to work
together on a science project.

Situation 5:
The students are
lined up to go outside.

Situation 6:
The students are
walking down the hall.

Situation 7:
In physical education class,
the group is learning
a new game.

Situation 8:
Everyone is in the
cafeteria, eating lunch.

Situation 9:
The class helper is returning papers.

CONQUERING BULLIES: LITTLE RASCALS SITUATION CARDS
© 2005 MAR∗CO PRODUCTS, INC. 1-800-448-2197

BULLY

CONQUERING BULLIES: LITTLE RASCALS BULLY CARDS
© 2005 MAR∗CO PRODUCTS, INC. 1-800-448-2197

CONQUERING BULLIES: LITTLE RASCALS BULLY CARDS
© 2005 MAR∗CO PRODUCTS, INC. 1-800-448-2197

CONQUERING BULLIES: LITTLE RASCALS BULLY CARDS
© 2005 MAR∗CO PRODUCTS, INC. 1-800-448-2197

CONQUERING BULLIES: LITTLE RASCALS BULLY CARDS
© 2005 MAR∗CO PRODUCTS, INC. 1-800-448-2197

CONQUERING BULLIES: LITTLE RASCALS BULLY CARDS
© 2005 MAR∗CO PRODUCTS, INC. 1-800-448-2197

CONQUERING BULLIES: LITTLE RASCALS BULLY CARDS
© 2005 MAR∗CO PRODUCTS, INC. 1-800-448-2197

CONQUERING BULLIES: LITTLE RASCALS BULLY CARDS
© 2005 MAR∗CO PRODUCTS, INC. 1-800-448-2197

IF YOU NEED TO ANSWER A BULLY
Sung to the tune of
If You're Happy And You Know It

If you need to answer a bully, **make a deal.**
If you need to answer a bully, **make a deal.**
If you need to answer a bully, use your wits to think it out.
If you need to answer a bully, **make a deal.**

If you need to answer a bully, **look surprised.**
If you need to answer a bully, **look surprised.**
If you need to answer a bully, act as if you can't believe it.
If you need to answer a bully, **look surprised.**

If you need to answer a bully, **yell out STOP!**
If you need to answer a bully, **yell out STOP!**
If you need to answer a bully, be firm and shout out loud.
If you need to answer a bully, **yell out STOP!**

If you need to answer a bully, **compliment.**
If you need to answer a bully, **compliment.**
If you need to answer a bully, say something very nice.
If you need to answer a bully, **compliment.**

If you need to answer a bully, just **agree.**
If you need to answer a bully, just **agree.**
If you need to answer a bully, and what is said is really right,
If you need to answer a bully, just **agree.**

If you need to answer a bully, just **ignore.**
If you need to answer a bully, just **ignore.**
If you need to answer a bully, just pretend he's/she's not there.
If you need to answer a bully, just **ignore.**

If you need to answer a bully, **make a joke.**
If you need to answer a bully, **make a joke.**
If you need to answer a bully, think of something funny.
If you need to answer a bully, **make a joke.**

POT SHOT STATEMENTS AND SITUATIONS

STATEMENTS:

You're a shrimp!

Hey, Fatty!

Get lost, Redhead!

Hey, teacher's pet! What are you gonna do next to get good grades?

How's the weather up there, tall girl?

I saw your big fat sister come to school with you.

I saw your house from the bus today. You sure live in a dump!

The picture you drew stinks.

Run, Slow Poke! Let's see how fast you can run.

Look at Four Eyes!

Fly away, Dumbo Ears.

Wow! They must be having a sale at the second-hand clothing store!

Miss Goodie Two Shoes!

SITUATIONS:

The bully pushes you away from the drinking fountain.

The bully grabs your dessert from your lunch tray.

You are threatened that something bad will happen if you don't give the bully your lunch money.

The bully pushes ahead of you in line.

In the restroom, the bully keeps opening the door on your stall.

On the playground, the bully chases and hits you.

ANSWERING THE BULLY
Sung to the tune of
Skip To My Lou

Laugh, laugh, laugh, make a joke.
Laugh, laugh, laugh, make a joke.
Laugh, laugh, laugh, make a joke.
Make a joke for the bully.

Yes, yes, yes, I agree.
Yes, yes, yes, I agree.
Yes, yes, yes, I agree.
I agree with the bully.

Sorry, sorry, yes I am.
Sorry, sorry, yes I am.
Sorry, sorry, yes I am.
Apologize to the bully.

What, what, what did you say?
What, what, what did you say?
What, what, what did you say?
You sure surprised me, Bully.

LOUD-MOUTH LION
GOSSIPING STATEMENTS

1. Susie sells seashells by the seashore.

2. The bear went over the mountain to see what he could see, but came back since there was nothing to see.

3. The skunk sat on a stump. The stump thought the skunk stunk and the skunk thought the stump stunk.

4. The horse came trotting and galloping at a fast pace back to the barn.

5. Every good man must come to the aid of his party.

6. The popcorn didn't pop because the popcorn popped open before it needed to do so.

7. The king and queen were happy to see the princess happy with a happy prince.

8. How much wood could a woodchuck chop if a woodchuck could chop wood?

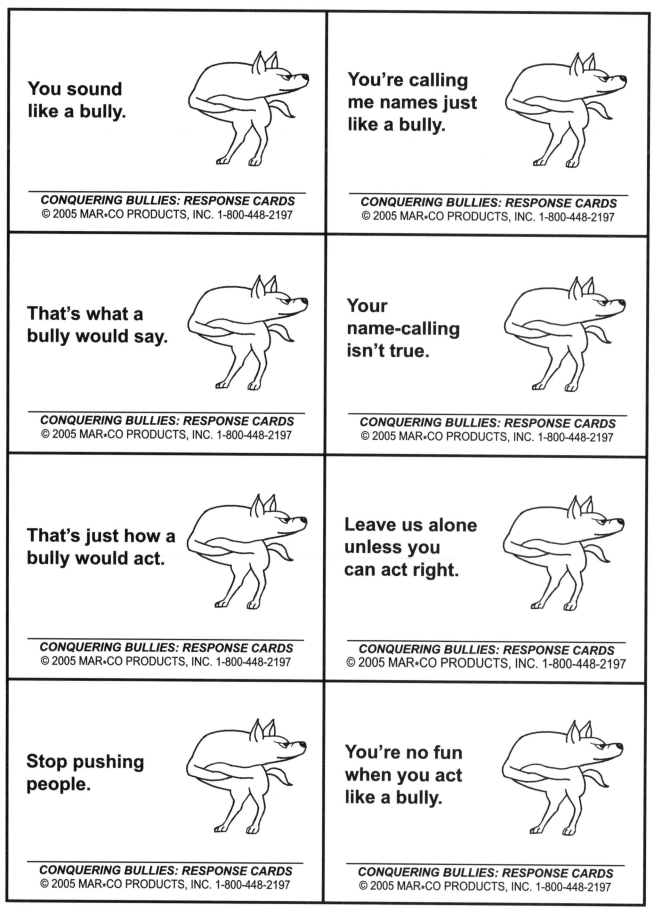

You sound
like a bully.

CONQUERING BULLIES: RESPONSE CARDS
© 2005 MAR∗CO PRODUCTS, INC. 1-800-448-2197

You're calling
me names just
like a bully.

CONQUERING BULLIES: RESPONSE CARDS
© 2005 MAR∗CO PRODUCTS, INC. 1-800-448-2197

That's what a
bully would say.

CONQUERING BULLIES: RESPONSE CARDS
© 2005 MAR∗CO PRODUCTS, INC. 1-800-448-2197

Your
name-calling
isn't true.

CONQUERING BULLIES: RESPONSE CARDS
© 2005 MAR∗CO PRODUCTS, INC. 1-800-448-2197

That's just how a
bully would act.

CONQUERING BULLIES: RESPONSE CARDS
© 2005 MAR∗CO PRODUCTS, INC. 1-800-448-2197

Leave us alone
unless you
can act right.

CONQUERING BULLIES: RESPONSE CARDS
© 2005 MAR∗CO PRODUCTS, INC. 1-800-448-2197

Stop pushing
people.

CONQUERING BULLIES: RESPONSE CARDS
© 2005 MAR∗CO PRODUCTS, INC. 1-800-448-2197

You're no fun
when you act
like a bully.

CONQUERING BULLIES: RESPONSE CARDS
© 2005 MAR∗CO PRODUCTS, INC. 1-800-448-2197

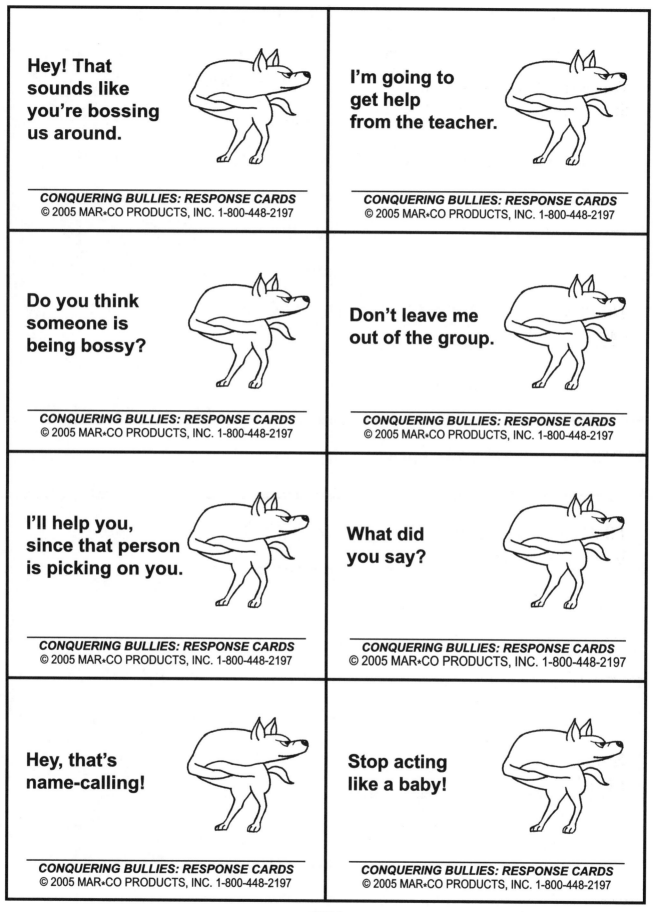

Hey! That sounds like you're bossing us around.

CONQUERING BULLIES: RESPONSE CARDS
© 2005 MAR∗CO PRODUCTS, INC. 1-800-448-2197

I'm going to get help from the teacher.

CONQUERING BULLIES: RESPONSE CARDS
© 2005 MAR∗CO PRODUCTS, INC. 1-800-448-2197

Do you think someone is being bossy?

CONQUERING BULLIES: RESPONSE CARDS
© 2005 MAR∗CO PRODUCTS, INC. 1-800-448-2197

Don't leave me out of the group.

CONQUERING BULLIES: RESPONSE CARDS
© 2005 MAR∗CO PRODUCTS, INC. 1-800-448-2197

I'll help you, since that person is picking on you.

CONQUERING BULLIES: RESPONSE CARDS
© 2005 MAR∗CO PRODUCTS, INC. 1-800-448-2197

What did you say?

CONQUERING BULLIES: RESPONSE CARDS
© 2005 MAR∗CO PRODUCTS, INC. 1-800-448-2197

Hey, that's name-calling!

CONQUERING BULLIES: RESPONSE CARDS
© 2005 MAR∗CO PRODUCTS, INC. 1-800-448-2197

Stop acting like a baby!

CONQUERING BULLIES: RESPONSE CARDS
© 2005 MAR∗CO PRODUCTS, INC. 1-800-448-2197

ZANY ZEBRA STATEMENTS

I didn't take your pencil.

I didn't lose the soccer ball. You were supposed to bring it in.

I'm not the only one who ran down the hall.

I didn't put that mess on your tray. You spit out your lunch.

No way! You didn't see me do anything.

I wasn't talking. You were talking to me. It's your fault.

That's not true. I didn't trip you. You just fell down.

I didn't copy your answers.

You said that bad word first.

I didn't call you *stupid*. *You* called me *stupid*.

I didn't say I didn't like the music teacher.
I said that I didn't like *music*.

Your mom is
too bossy.

CONQUERING BULLIES: ERUPTING ELEPHANT CARDS
© 2005 MAR∗CO PRODUCTS, INC. 1-800-448-2197

You've got an ugly,
old house.

CONQUERING BULLIES: ERUPTING ELEPHANT CARDS
© 2005 MAR∗CO PRODUCTS, INC. 1-800-448-2197

Nobody
likes you.

CONQUERING BULLIES: ERUPTING ELEPHANT CARDS
© 2005 MAR∗CO PRODUCTS, INC. 1-800-448-2197

Don't play with us.
Go somewhere
else to play.

CONQUERING BULLIES: ERUPTING ELEPHANT CARDS
© 2005 MAR∗CO PRODUCTS, INC. 1-800-448-2197

With that big
hooked nose, you
might catch a fish.

CONQUERING BULLIES: ERUPTING ELEPHANT CARDS
© 2005 MAR∗CO PRODUCTS, INC. 1-800-448-2197

I don't like
that hairdo.

CONQUERING BULLIES: ERUPTING ELEPHANT CARDS
© 2005 MAR∗CO PRODUCTS, INC. 1-800-448-2197

Those are big,
ugly glasses
that you've got on.

CONQUERING BULLIES: ERUPTING ELEPHANT CARDS
© 2005 MAR∗CO PRODUCTS, INC. 1-800-448-2197

He's got cooties.

CONQUERING BULLIES: ERUPTING ELEPHANT CARDS
© 2005 MAR∗CO PRODUCTS, INC. 1-800-448-2197

You're too
little to play.

CONQUERING BULLIES: ERUPTING ELEPHANT CARDS
© 2005 MAR∗CO PRODUCTS, INC. 1-800-448-2197

You're not very
smart. You always
get bad grades.

CONQUERING BULLIES: ERUPTING ELEPHANT CARDS
© 2005 MAR∗CO PRODUCTS, INC. 1-800-448-2197

Why doesn't your
dad work?
Is he too lazy?

CONQUERING BULLIES: ERUPTING ELEPHANT CARDS
© 2005 MAR∗CO PRODUCTS, INC. 1-800-448-2197

My dad makes
more money
than your dad does.

CONQUERING BULLIES: ERUPTING ELEPHANT CARDS
© 2005 MAR∗CO PRODUCTS, INC. 1-800-448-2197

CONQUERING BULLIES © 2005 MAR∗CO PRODUCTS, INC. 1-800-448-2197

Look at those big
ears that you've got.

CONQUERING BULLIES: ERUPTING ELEPHANT CARDS
© 2005 MAR*CO PRODUCTS, INC. 1-800-448-2197

Why are
you so fat?

CONQUERING BULLIES: ERUPTING ELEPHANT CARDS
© 2005 MAR*CO PRODUCTS, INC. 1-800-448-2197

Thank you
for inviting me.

CONQUERING BULLIES: ERUPTING ELEPHANT CARDS
© 2005 MAR*CO PRODUCTS, INC. 1-800-448-2197

Please pass
the salt.

CONQUERING BULLIES: ERUPTING ELEPHANT CARDS
© 2005 MAR*CO PRODUCTS, INC. 1-800-448-2197

When I sneeze,
I use a tissue.

CONQUERING BULLIES: ERUPTING ELEPHANT CARDS
© 2005 MAR*CO PRODUCTS, INC. 1-800-448-2197

No, thank you.
I don't care
for any candy.

CONQUERING BULLIES: ERUPTING ELEPHANT CARDS
© 2005 MAR*CO PRODUCTS, INC. 1-800-448-2197

You have
nice hair.

CONQUERING BULLIES: ERUPTING ELEPHANT CARDS
© 2005 MAR*CO PRODUCTS, INC. 1-800-448-2197

Come play
with us.

CONQUERING BULLIES: ERUPTING ELEPHANT CARDS
© 2005 MAR*CO PRODUCTS, INC. 1-800-448-2197

You played a
really good game.

CONQUERING BULLIES: ERUPTING ELEPHANT CARDS
© 2005 MAR*CO PRODUCTS, INC. 1-800-448-2197

Wow! An "A" on
your math test.
That's great!

CONQUERING BULLIES: ERUPTING ELEPHANT CARDS
© 2005 MAR*CO PRODUCTS, INC. 1-800-448-2197

Thank you for
helping me with
my science project.

CONQUERING BULLIES: ERUPTING ELEPHANT CARDS
© 2005 MAR*CO PRODUCTS, INC. 1-800-448-2197

May I borrow
a pencil, please?

CONQUERING BULLIES: ERUPTING ELEPHANT CARDS
© 2005 MAR*CO PRODUCTS, INC. 1-800-448-2197

Hey, Four Eyes!

Is this the Creep Show?

Hello, Fatso!

Hello, Lazy!

Is this the klutz who made us lose the game?

Hi, Big Feet!

Hey, Stupid!

Freckle Face! Freckle Face!

Nerd.

Smarty.

Big Ears, Big Ears!

Hey, Loser!

CONQUERING BULLIES: HARASSING HIPPO CARDS
© 2005 MAR∗CO PRODUCTS, INC. 1-800-448-2197

CONQUERING BULLIES: HARASSING HIPPO CARDS
© 2005 MAR∗CO PRODUCTS, INC. 1-800-448-2197

CONQUERING BULLIES: HARASSING HIPPO CARDS
© 2005 MAR∗CO PRODUCTS, INC. 1-800-448-2197

CONQUERING BULLIES: HARASSING HIPPO CARDS
© 2005 MAR∗CO PRODUCTS, INC. 1-800-448-2197

CONQUERING BULLIES: HARASSING HIPPO CARDS
© 2005 MAR∗CO PRODUCTS, INC. 1-800-448-2197

CONQUERING BULLIES: HARASSING HIPPO CARDS
© 2005 MAR∗CO PRODUCTS, INC. 1-800-448-2197

CONQUERING BULLIES: HARASSING HIPPO CARDS
© 2005 MAR∗CO PRODUCTS, INC. 1-800-448-2197

CONQUERING BULLIES: HARASSING HIPPO CARDS
© 2005 MAR∗CO PRODUCTS, INC. 1-800-448-2197

CONQUERING BULLIES: HARASSING HIPPO CARDS
© 2005 MAR∗CO PRODUCTS, INC. 1-800-448-2197

CONQUERING BULLIES: HARASSING HIPPO CARDS
© 2005 MAR∗CO PRODUCTS, INC. 1-800-448-2197

CONQUERING BULLIES: HARASSING HIPPO CARDS
© 2005 MAR∗CO PRODUCTS, INC. 1-800-448-2197

CONQUERING BULLIES: HARASSING HIPPO CARDS
© 2005 MAR∗CO PRODUCTS, INC. 1-800-448-2197

REFUSING RHINO STATEMENTS
(Mix up the statements as they are called out.)

Note: Many of the statements under the *Spot The Bully Station* and *Confront Station* are interchangeable. The leader should decide if he/she will accept either station as a correct decision.

SPOT THE BULLY STATION:
Be alert! Recognize a bully's actions or words.
 What did you say?
 Did you mean to lie about what happened?
 Did you think before you put the blame on someone else?
 That's a lie!
 You're lying, so you must be a bully.
 You know better than to lie like that, don't you?

CONFRONT STATION:
Confront the bully. Tell the bully what he/she said or did.
 Why are you lying?
 Did you mean to blame me for something you did?
 That's not true.
 Don't blame somebody else for something you did.
 You must be awfully scared to blame somebody else for something you did.
 I saw you do that.
 That's a lie, and that's not nice.
 What you're doing is bullying.
 That's a lie, not the truth.
 You can lie all you want, but the truth is that you stole the lunch money.

CONFIRM TEAM STATION:
Confirm what the bully is doing or talk about it with others.
 Do you think he/she is lying?
 Did you see what I saw him/her do?
 Did you hear what he/she said before? Isn't that different than what he/she is saying now?
 Do you think that was his/her fault?
 That sounds like a lie. What do the rest of you think?
 Does that sound like lying to the rest of you?

HELP STATION:
Support and help others. Be there for others if they are being bullied.
 Don't tell lies about my friend.
 Stop trying to blame him/her.
 We need to go to the teacher and tell the truth.
 Your mom won't like that you're telling lies about her/him.
 It's not fair that you lied and got him/her in trouble.
 Don't blame him/her for something you did.

177

SNAPPY SNAKE
Sung to the tune of
She'll Be Comin' Round The Mountain

Snappy will be comin' 'round the mountain when she comes.
Snappy will be comin' 'round the mountain when she comes.
She'll be comin' 'round the mountain,
She'll be comin' 'round the mountain,
Snappy will be comin' 'round the mountain when she comes.

She'll be pushin' and a shovin' when she comes.
She'll be pushin' and a shovin' when she comes.
She'll be pushin' and a shovin',
She'll be pushin' and a shovin',
She'll be pushin' and a shovin' when she comes.

She'll be kickin' and a spittin' when she comes.
She'll be kickin' and a spittin' when she comes.
She'll be kickin' and a spittin',
She'll be kickin' and a spittin',
She'll be kickin' and a spittin' when she comes.

She'll be fussin' and a fumin' when she comes.
She'll be fussin' and a fumin' when she comes.
She'll be fussin' and a fumin',
She'll be fussin' and a fumin',
She'll be fussin' and a fumin' when she comes.

SNAPPY SNAKE SITUATION CARD #1

SKIT: ON THE BEACH

Child 1:   Let's go swimming in the ocean.

Child 2:   I've got a float and some flippers.

Child 3:   Those flippers are dumb.

Child 2:   No, they're not. I think it sounds like fun. Let's go.

Child 3:   (Whining) But I won't have anything to do if you go swimming.

Child 1:   Then come with us.

Child 3:   No! I don't want to be seen with you and those ugly flippers.

SNAPPY SNAKE SITUATION CARD #2

SKIT: THE PARTY

Child 1:   Why can't we have cake and ice cream now? I'm hungry.

Child 2:   We have to wait until Sam gets here.

Child 1:   I'm tired of waiting. It's no fair!

Child 2:   Yeah, but Sam called and asked us to wait for him since his dad was running late.

Child 1:   I don't care. I'm hungry NOW!

Child 3:   Well, as long as we're waiting, let's play a board game until Sam gets here.

Child 1:   I'm no good at board games. I don't want to do that. I want some cake and ice cream.

Child 3:   I'm sure Sam will be here soon.

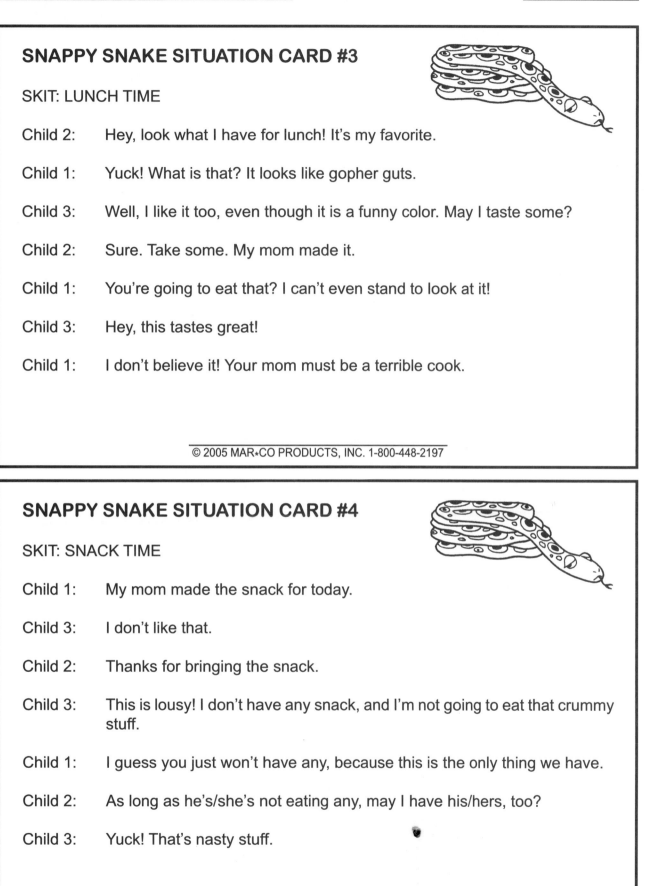

SNAPPY SNAKE SITUATION CARD #3

SKIT: LUNCH TIME

Child 2:   Hey, look what I have for lunch! It's my favorite.

Child 1:   Yuck! What is that? It looks like gopher guts.

Child 3:   Well, I like it too, even though it is a funny color. May I taste some?

Child 2:   Sure. Take some. My mom made it.

Child 1:   You're going to eat that? I can't even stand to look at it!

Child 3:   Hey, this tastes great!

Child 1:   I don't believe it! Your mom must be a terrible cook.

SNAPPY SNAKE SITUATION CARD #4

SKIT: SNACK TIME

Child 1:   My mom made the snack for today.

Child 3:   I don't like that.

Child 2:   Thanks for bringing the snack.

Child 3:   This is lousy! I don't have any snack, and I'm not going to eat that crummy stuff.

Child 1:   I guess you just won't have any, because this is the only thing we have.

Child 2:   As long as he's/she's not eating any, may I have his/hers, too?

Child 3:   Yuck! That's nasty stuff.

SNAPPY SNAKE SITUATION CARD #5

SKIT: THE PROJECT

Child 3:   The teacher wants us to make a volcano for a science project.

Child 2:   OK. I can get some paint.

Child 1:   Our teacher's dumb. Volcanoes are stupid.

Child 3:   I'm going to get some clay. We can paint it after we build the volcano.

Child 1:   BORING!

Child 2:   Come and help us. You can make some trees and houses falling down when the lava hits them.

Child 1:   I don't want to do stupid trees and houses. I'm going to make something different than a volcano, anyway.

Child 3:   But we all will be getting graded on this project together. You'd better help.

Child 1:   Bug off! I'll do it my way. I don't care.

© 2005 MAR∗CO PRODUCTS, INC. 1-800-448-2197

SNAPPY SNAKE SITUATION CARD #6

SKIT: LIBRARY TIME

Child 1:   I need this new book.

Child 2:   So do I. Give it to me.

Child 1:   No! This is the one I need to get.

Child 2:   That's not fair. I saw it first.

Child 3:   Here's another one. Why don't you look at it? It's all about soccer, too.

Child 2:   No! I want that one. Give it to me now, or I'll tell.

Child 1:   I guess you'll have to tell, because I'm checking this one out.

Child 2:   (Crying) You're being mean to me! I'm not your friend any more.

Child 3:   Look at all of the books in this library. Just be reasonable and get another book until that one is returned.

© 2005 MAR∗CO PRODUCTS, INC. 1-800-448-2197

SNAPPY SNAKE SITUATION CARD #7

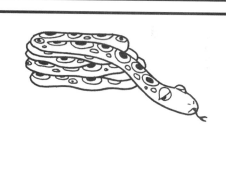

SKIT: THE BALL GAME

Child 3:   I'm going to be captain! That makes *me* first in line.

Child 1:   Well, why don't we do it in a fair way by flipping a coin and calling "heads" or "tails?"

Child 2:   You're always the captain, and we never get a turn. You always do things first.

Child 3:   I'm not going to play if I can't be captain. And if I don't play, I don't care. You are lousy players, anyway.

Child 1:   Then I guess we'll play without you. Come on, everybody.

Child 2:   Wait! Let's do *Rock Paper Scissors* to see who gets to be captain.

Child 3:   But if someone else is captain, they will never be as good as I am. I'm telling the teacher how you are treating me.

Child 1:   Go on and tell if you want to. Or you can join us in choosing a captain with *Rock Paper Scissors.*

SNAPPY SNAKE SITUATION CARD #8

SKIT: DRINKING FOUNTAIN

Child 1:   Get out of my way!

Child 2:   No way! It's my turn.

Child 3:   Don't push! There's plenty of water for everyone.

Child 1:   I don't care. I want to be first. Move!

Child 2:   But that's not fair!

Child 1:   I don't care.

Child 3:   You're acting as if you're more important than anybody else.

Child 1:   Well, maybe I am!

SNAPPY SNAKE SITUATION CARD #9

SKIT: RECESS: TWO TEACHERS TALKING

Teacher 1: What are you doing in your class?

Teacher 2: We're studying dinosaurs. What is your class studying?

Child 3: Mrs. Smith, look at this cut on my finger from two weeks ago. It's going away.

Teacher 1: You need to wait your turn. I'm speaking with another adult.

Child 3: But I need to talk with you.

Teacher 2: Be patient, and you will get to talk with me.

SNAPPY SNAKE SITUATION CARD #10

SKIT: INTERCOM

Person 1: (Speaking on intercom) Attention, students! This is a very important announcement.

Child 2: I need to sharpen my pencil.

Teacher 3: Please don't talk.

Child 2: He took my pencil.

Teacher 3: I can't hear! Please be quiet!

Person 1: (Speaking on intercom) Teachers, send this to the office now. Thank you.

Teacher 3: Now I don't know what I am supposed to do.

Don't Be A Loud-Mouth Lion!

GOSSIPING AND LYING IS HURTFUL.

Neji, you can't play any more.

Don't Be A Hurtful Hyena!
INCLUDE OTHERS IN GROUPS AND GAMES.

Don't Be A Tyrannical Tiger!

DON'T BE BOSSY AND TELL OTHERS WHAT TO DO.

188

Don't Be A Zany Zebra!

WHEN YOU DO SOMETHING WRONG, ADMIT IT.

189

Don't Be An Erupting Elephant!

NEVER PUT-DOWN OR MAKE FUN OF OTHERS.

Don't Be A Gloating Giraffe!

DON'T ACT AS IF YOU ARE BETTER THAN OTHERS.

191

STOP!

Don't Be A Menacing Monkey!
NEVER GANG UP AGAINST OTHERS.

Don't Be A Harassing Hippo!

NAME-CALLING IS HURTFUL.

Don't Be A Refusing Rhino!

DON'T BLAME OTHERS FOR YOUR WRONGDOING.

194

Don't Be A Snappy Snake!

USE GOOD MANNERS. DON'T WHINE AND COMPLAIN.

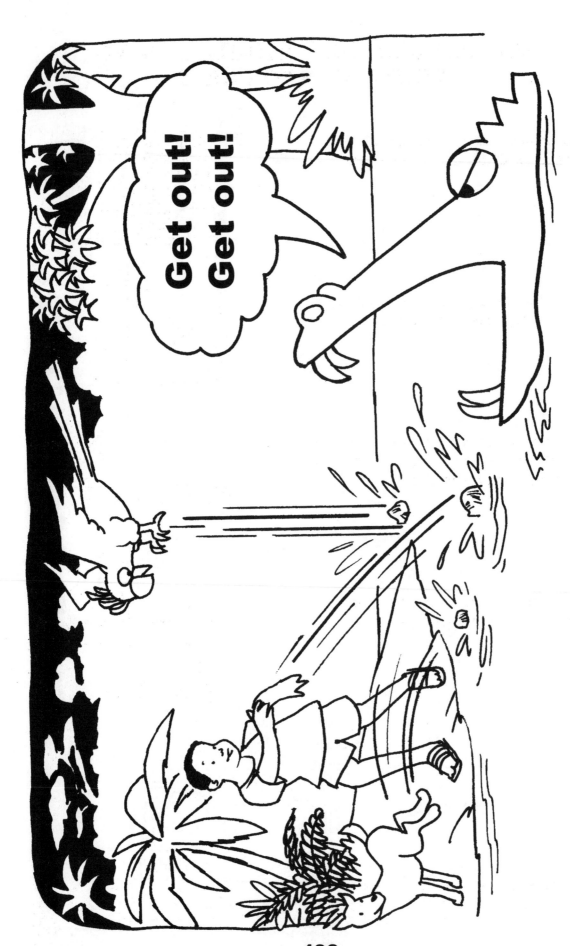

Don't Be A Croaking Crocodile!

DON'T YELL AT OTHERS.

PAPER JUNGLE ANIMAL HATS
DIRECTIONS FOR HATS

1. On the already creased fold, fold a full-page newspaper or 21.5" x 25" piece of paper in half.

2. With the fold on top, fold the top corners down until they meet in the middle.

3. Fold the bottom up on both sides. If the hat is too large, continue folding the bottom up until it is the appropriate size.

4. Cut off the ends of the bottom band and fold the band up again on both sides.

5. Tuck the ends of the band in on both sides and glue them in place.

6. Attach pattern pieces as described in the individual pattern directions

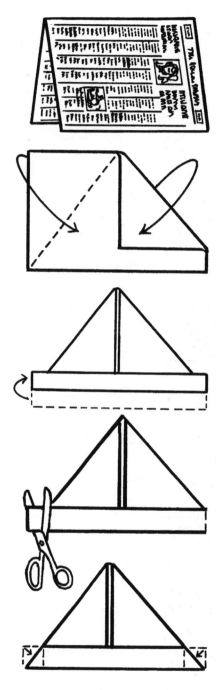

LOUD-MOUTH LION HAT

Directions:

1. Make a newspaper hat (see page 197).

2. Reproduce all the required pattern pieces on medium-weight colored paper.

   Suggested colors:

   Head: tan or gold
   Mane: gold
   Eyes: white
   Teeth: white

   Alternative: Reproduce the pattern pieces on medium- weight white paper and color them.

   Squiggly eyes, glitter, yarn, ribbon, etc. may also be used to decorate the hat.

3. Cut out the pattern pieces.

4. Glue the pattern pieces as shown in the above picture to both sides of the hat.

LOUD-MOUTH LION
HAT PATTERN

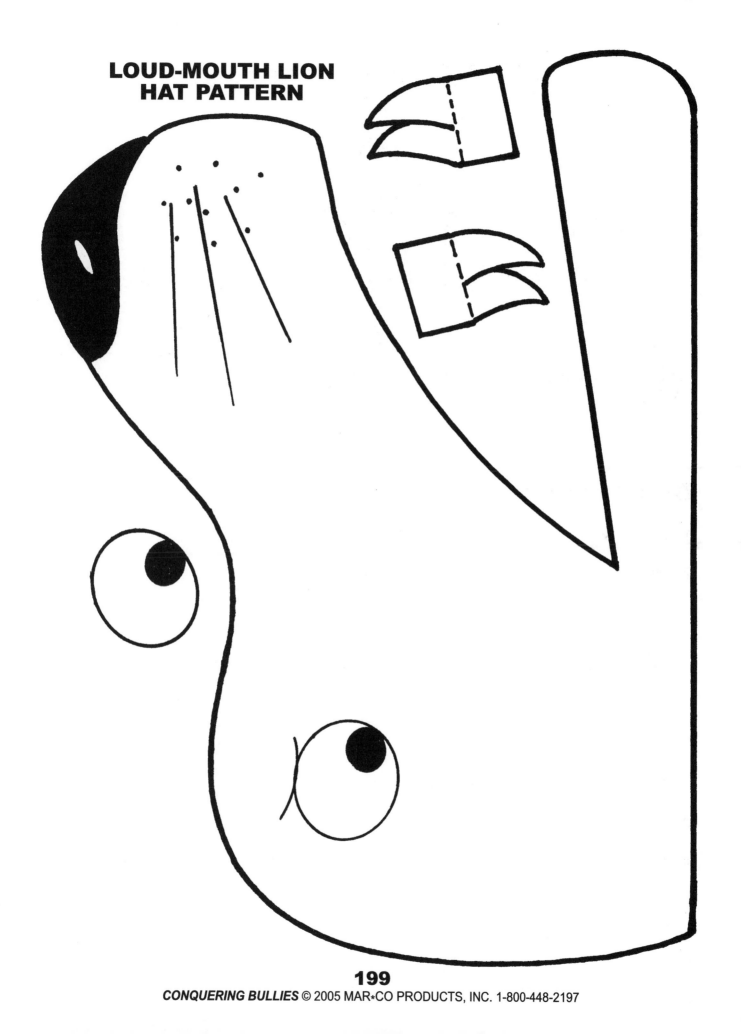

199

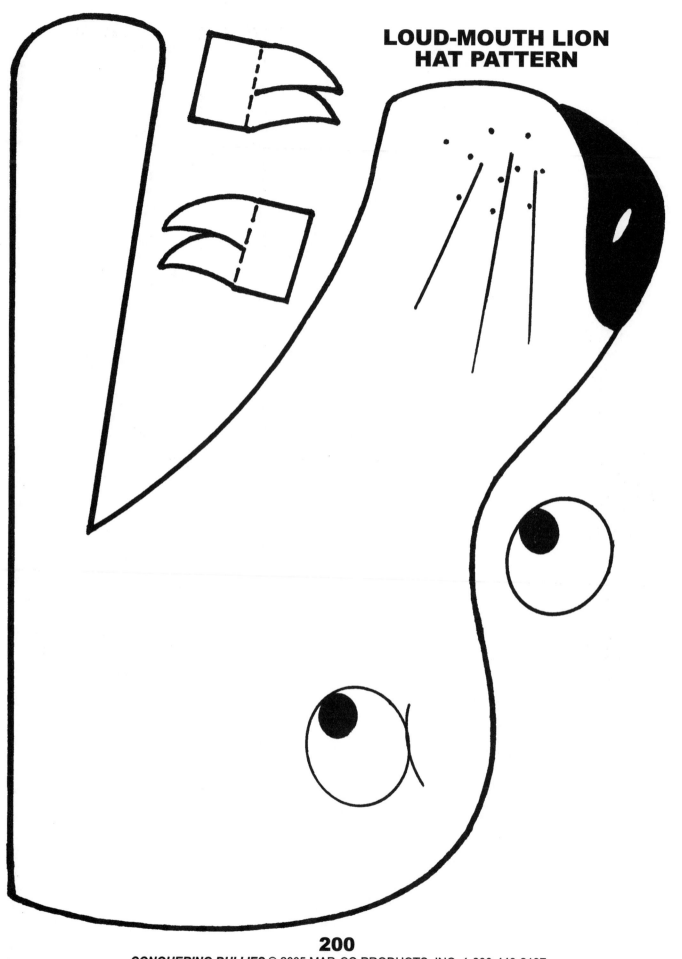

LOUD-MOUTH LION HAT PATTERN

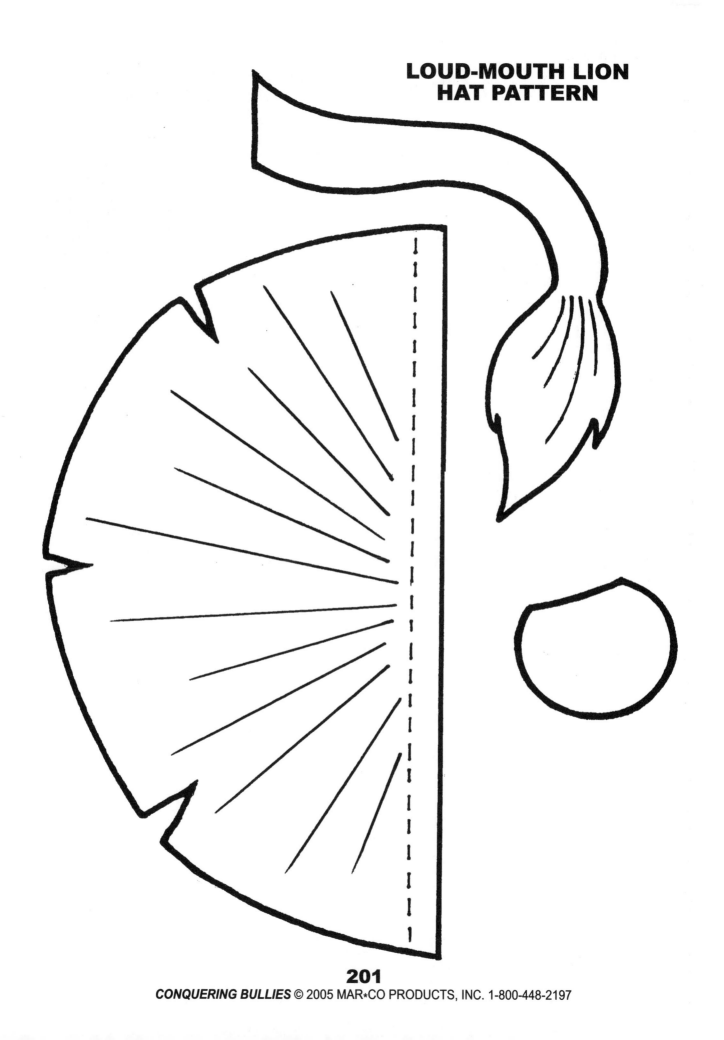

LOUD-MOUTH LION
HAT PATTERN

LOUD-MOUTH LION
HAT PATTERN

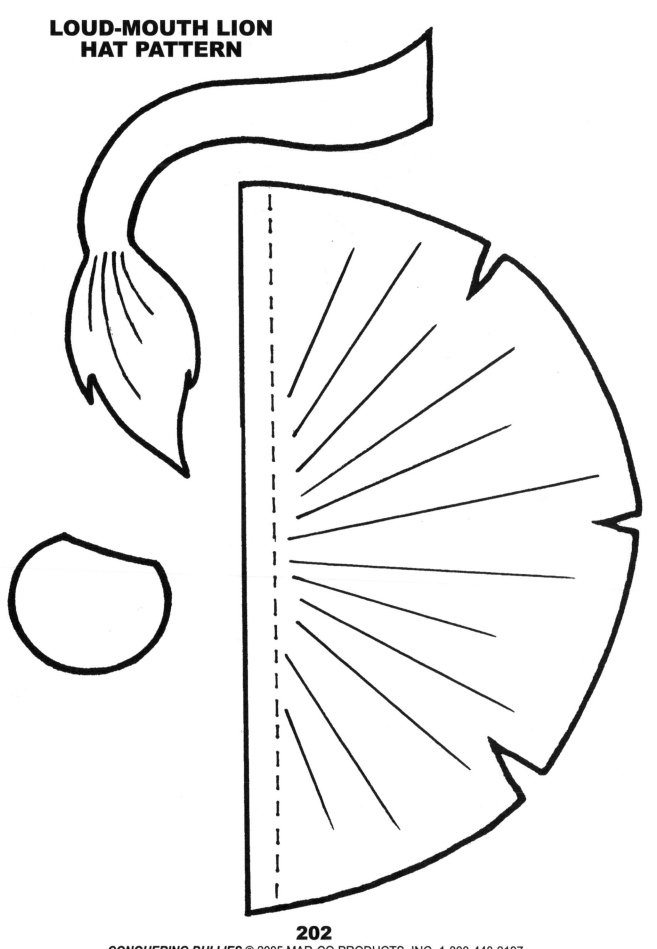

202

HURTFUL HYENA HAT

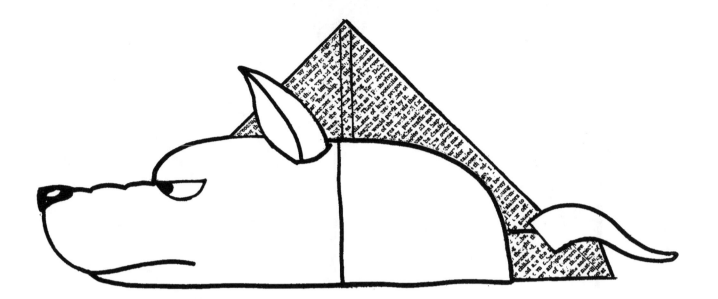

Directions:

1. Make a newspaper hat (see page 197).

2. Reproduce all the required pattern pieces on medium-weight colored paper.

   Suggested colors:

   Head: tan or gray
   Tail: tan or gray
   Eyes: white

   Alternative: Reproduce the pattern pieces on medium- weight white paper and color them.

   Squiggly eyes, glitter, yarn, ribbon, etc. may also be used to decorate the hat.

3. Cut out the pattern pieces.

4. Glue the pattern pieces as shown in the above picture to both sides of the hat.

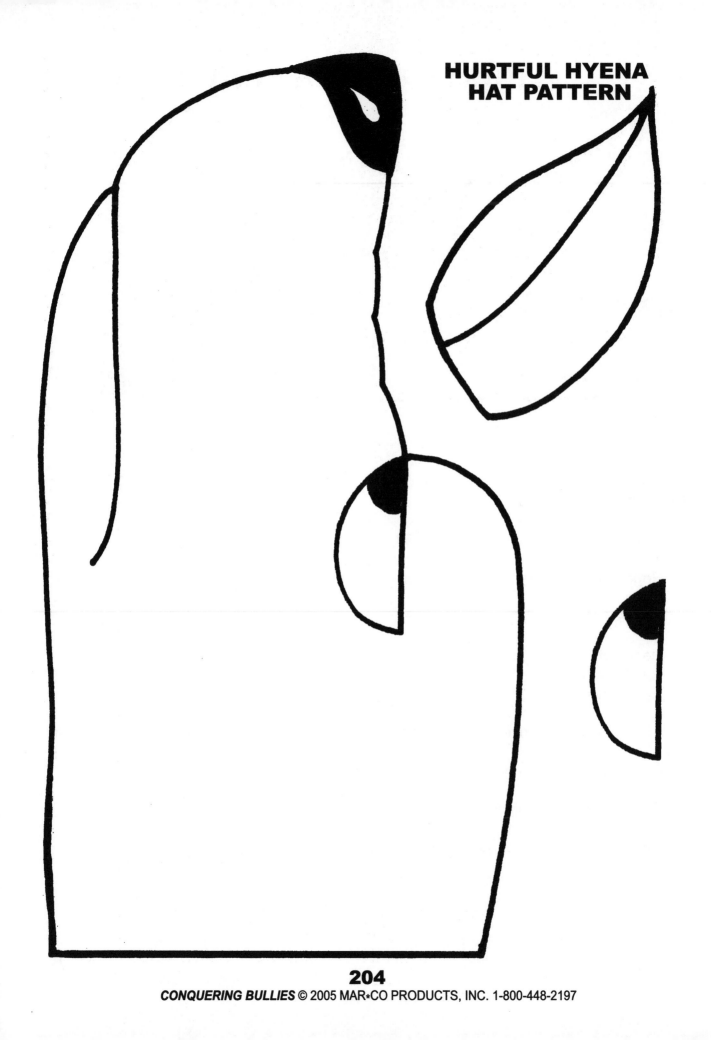

**HURTFUL HYENA
HAT PATTERN**

HURTFUL HYENA
HAT PATTERN

HURTFUL HYENA
HAT PATTERN

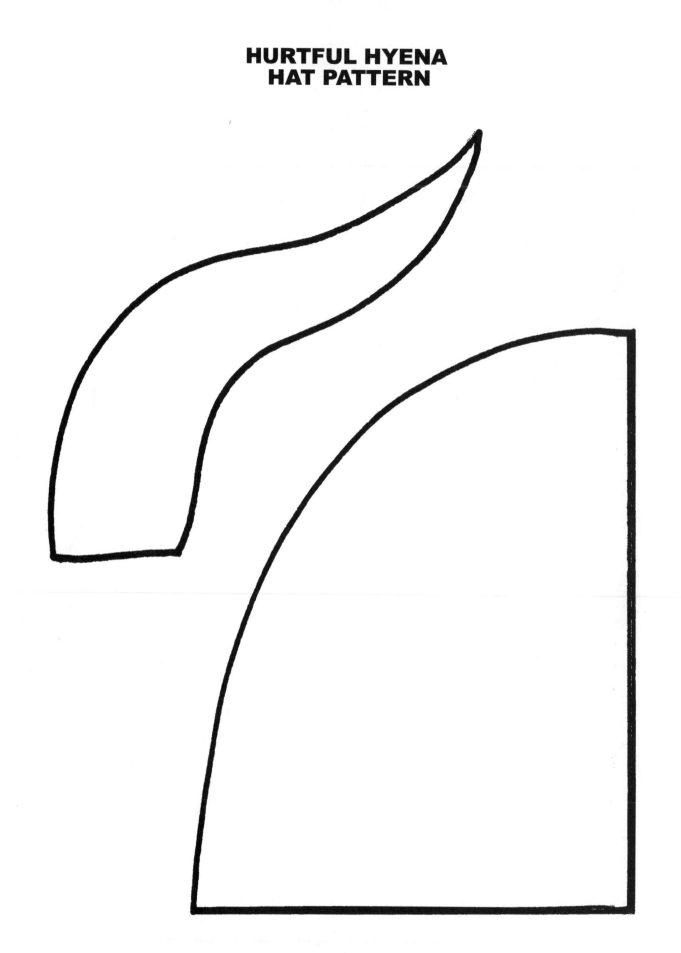

HURTFUL HYENA
HAT PATTERN

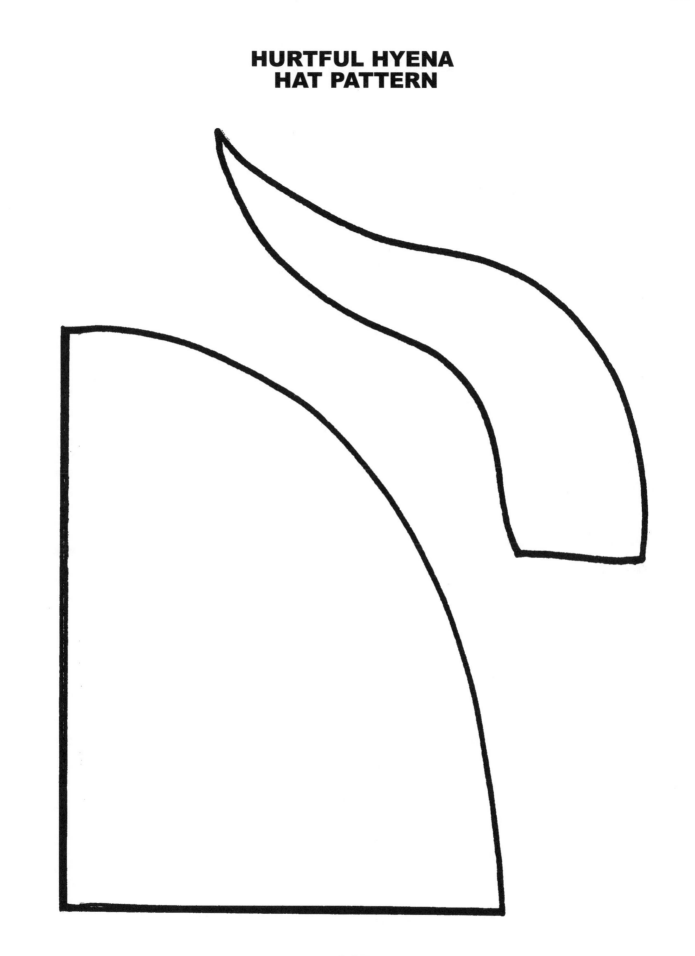

WALLOPING WARTHOG HAT

Directions:

1. Make a newspaper hat (see page 197).

2. Reproduce all the required pattern pieces on medium-weight colored paper.

   Suggested colors:

   Head: tan or gray
   Tail: tan or gray
   Eyes: white
   Horns: white

   Alternative: Reproduce the pattern pieces on medium- weight white paper and color them.

   Squiggly eyes, glitter, yarn, ribbon, etc. may also be used to decorate the hat.

3. Cut out the pattern pieces.

4. Glue the pattern pieces as shown in the above picture to both sides of the hat.

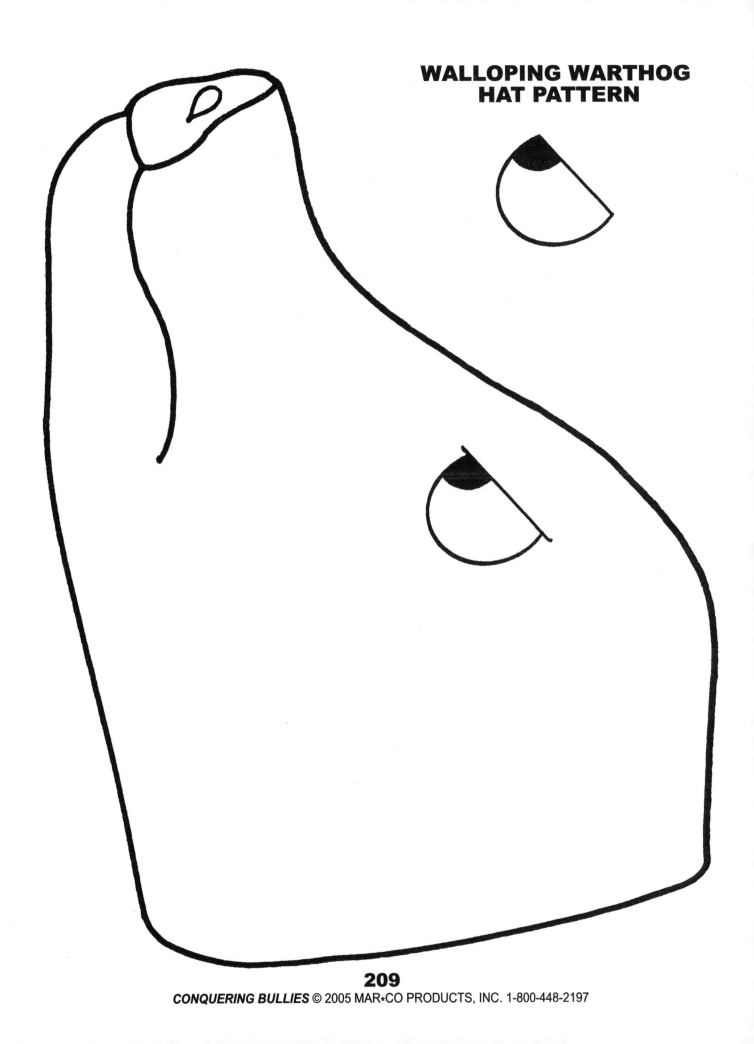

WALLOPING WARTHOG HAT PATTERN

WALLOPING WARTHOG
HAT PATTERN

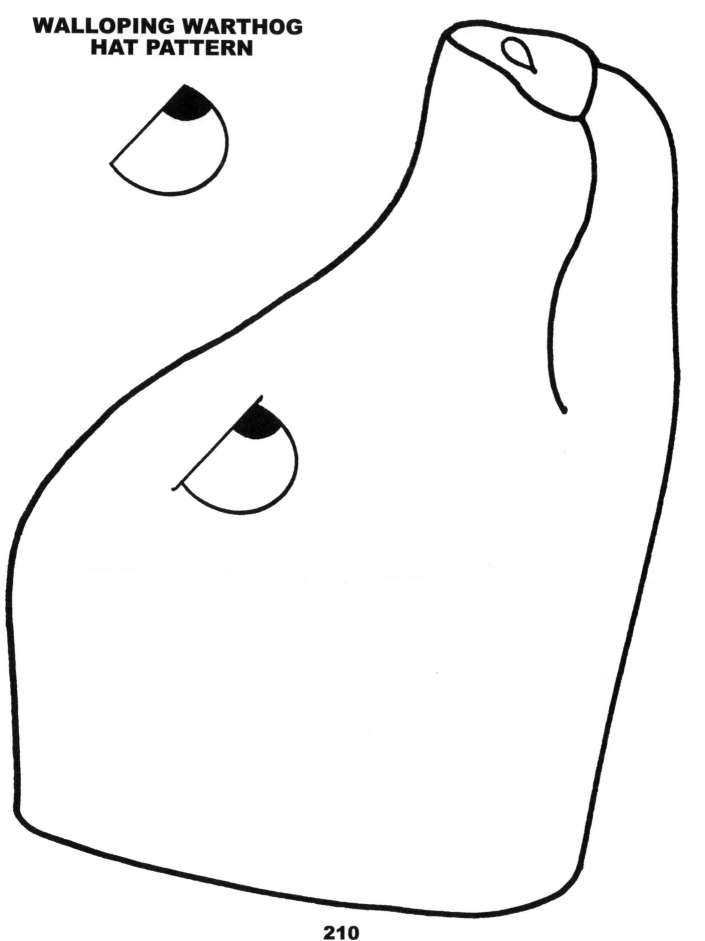

210

WALLOPING WARTHOG
HAT PATTERN

TYRANNICAL TIGER HAT

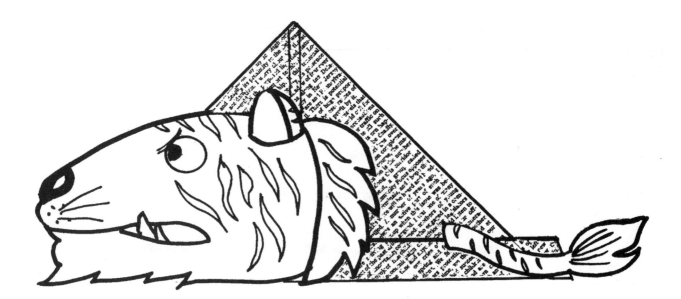

Directions:

1. Make a newspaper hat (see page 197).

2. Reproduce all the required pattern pieces on medium-weight colored paper.

   Suggested colors:

   Head: gold
   Tail: gold
   Eyes: white

   Alternative: Reproduce the pattern pieces on medium- weight white paper and color them.

   Squiggly eyes, glitter, yarn, ribbon, etc. may also be used to decorate the hat.

3. Cut out the pattern pieces.

4. Glue the pattern pieces as shown in the above picture to both sides of the hat.

TYRANNICAL TIGER
HAT PATTERN

213

TYRANNICAL TIGER
HAT PATTERN

TYRANNICAL TIGER
HAT PATTERN

TYRANNICAL TIGER HAT PATTERN

ZANY ZEBRA HAT

Directions:

1. Make a newspaper hat (see page 197).

2. Reproduce all the required pattern pieces on medium-weight paper.

   Suggested colors:

   Head: white
   Mane: white
   Tail: white
   Eyes: white

   Alternative: Reproduce the pattern pieces on medium- weight white paper and color them.

   Squiggly eyes, glitter, yarn, ribbon, etc. may also be used to decorate the hat.

3. Cut out the pattern pieces.

4. Glue the pattern pieces as shown in the above picture to both sides of the hat.

ZANY ZEBRA
HAT PATTERN

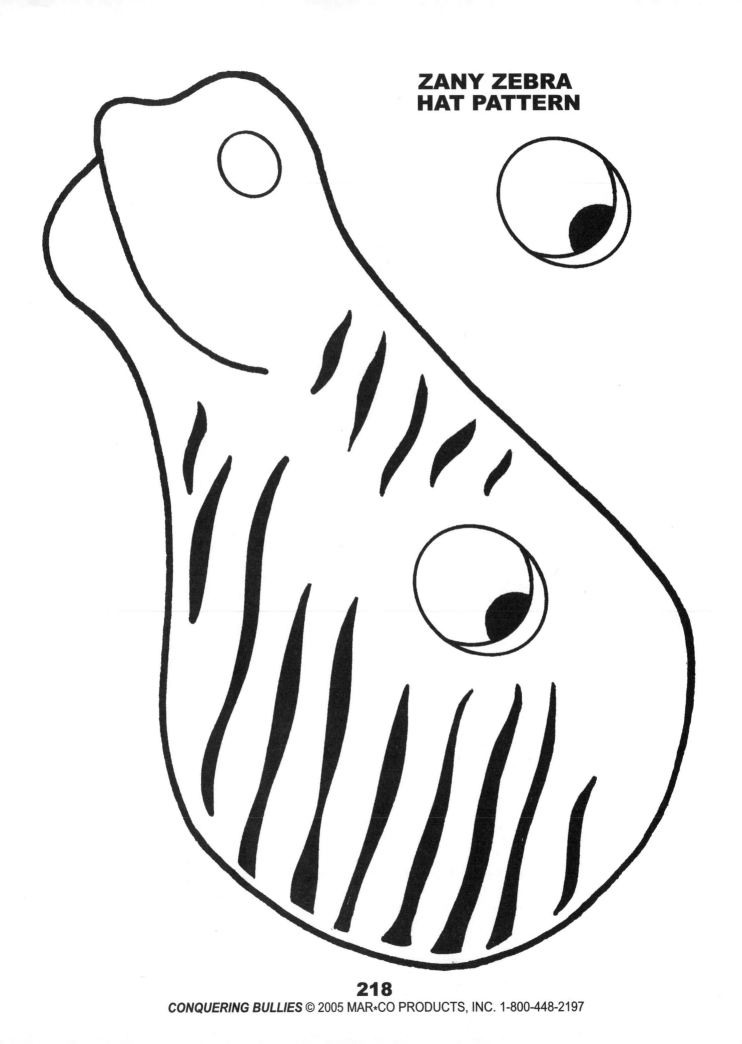

218

ZANY ZEBRA
HAT PATTERN

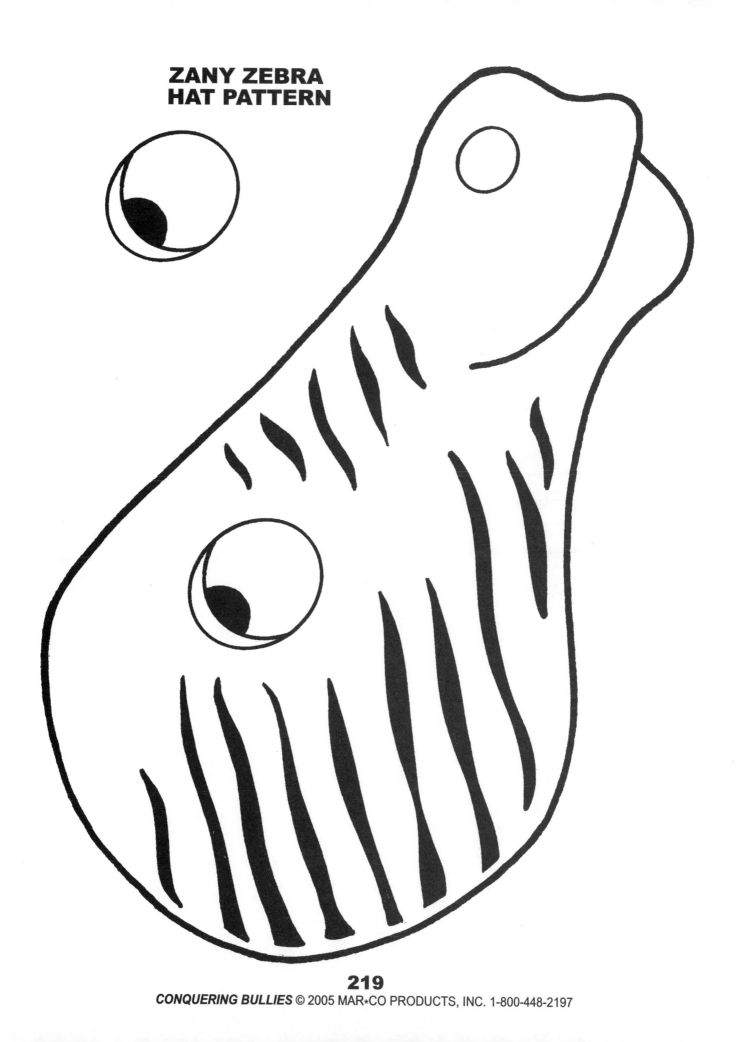

ZANY ZEBRA
HAT PATTERN

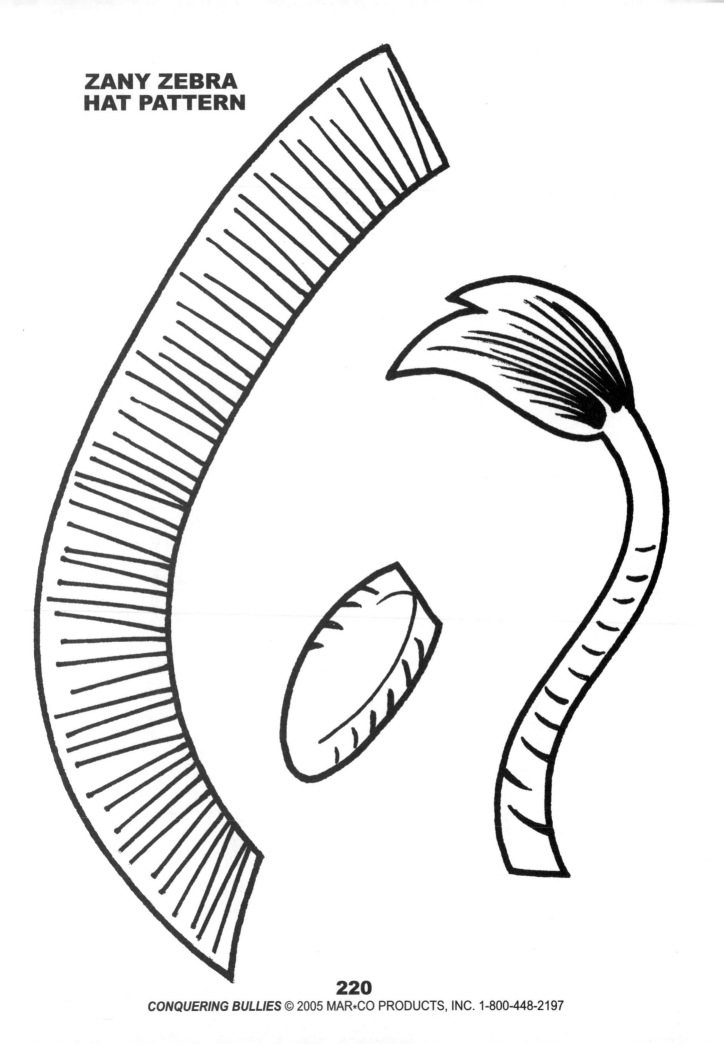

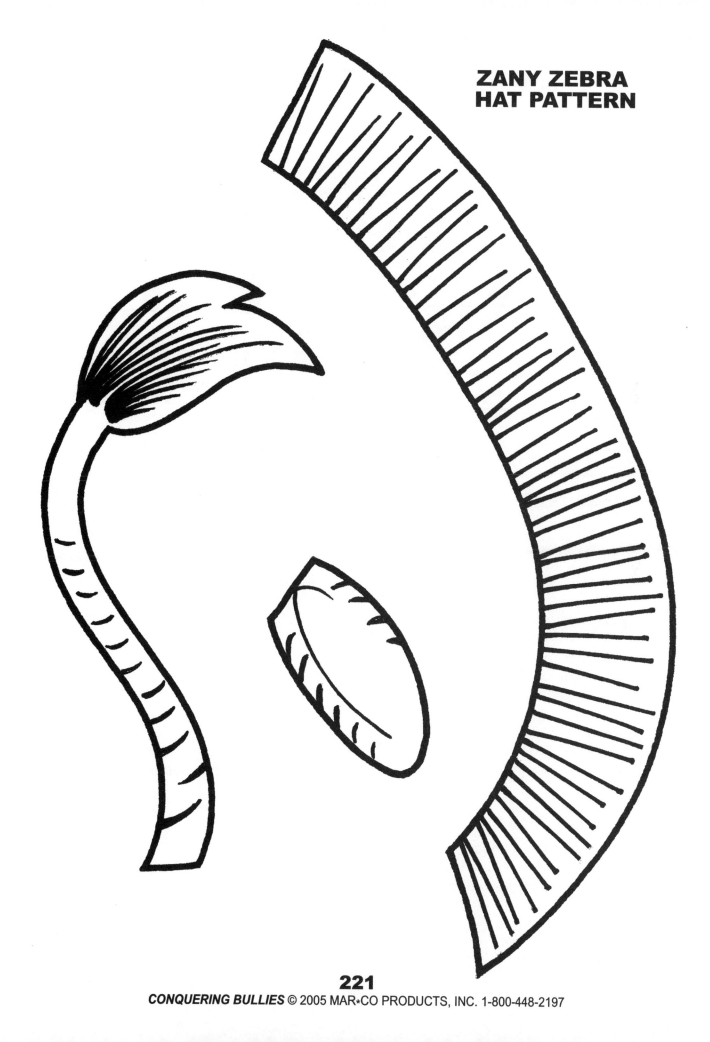

ZANY ZEBRA HAT PATTERN

ERUPTING ELEPHANT HAT

Directions:

1. Make a newspaper hat (see page 197).

2. Reproduce all the required pattern pieces on medium-weight colored paper.

    Suggested colors:

    Head: gray or purple
    Trunk: gray or purple
    Tail: gray or purple
    Tusks: white
    Eyes: white

    Alternative: Reproduce the pattern pieces on medium- weight white paper and color them.

    Squiggly eyes, glitter, yarn, ribbon, etc. may also be used to decorate the hat.

3. Cut out the pattern pieces.

4. Glue the pattern pieces as shown in the above picture to both sides of the hat.

ERUPTING ELEPHANT
HAT PATTERN

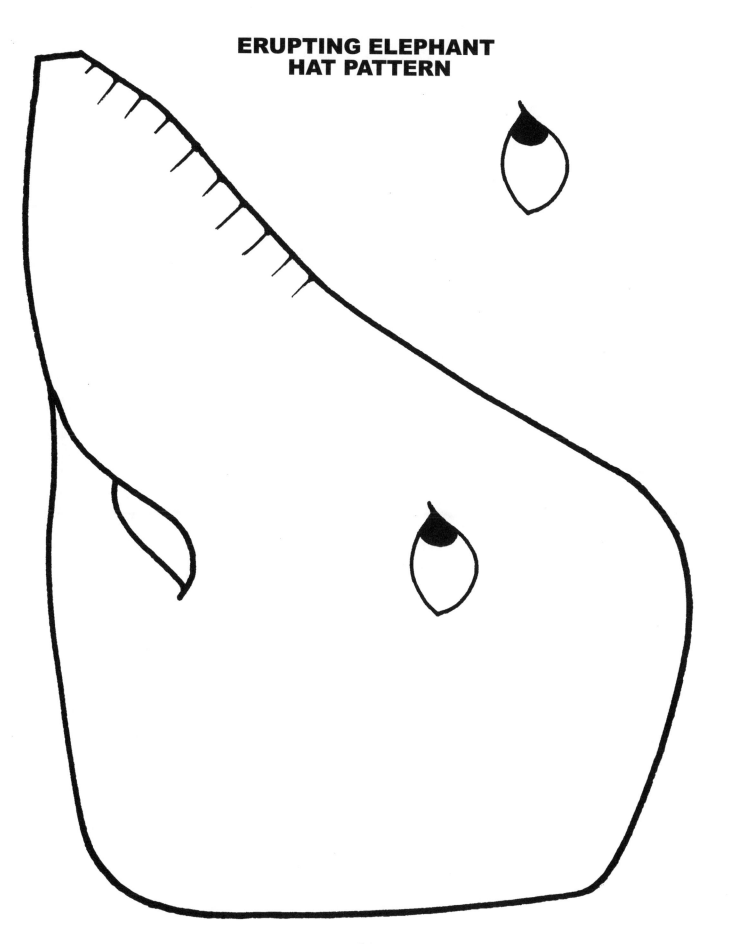

ERUPTING ELEPHANT
HAT PATTERN

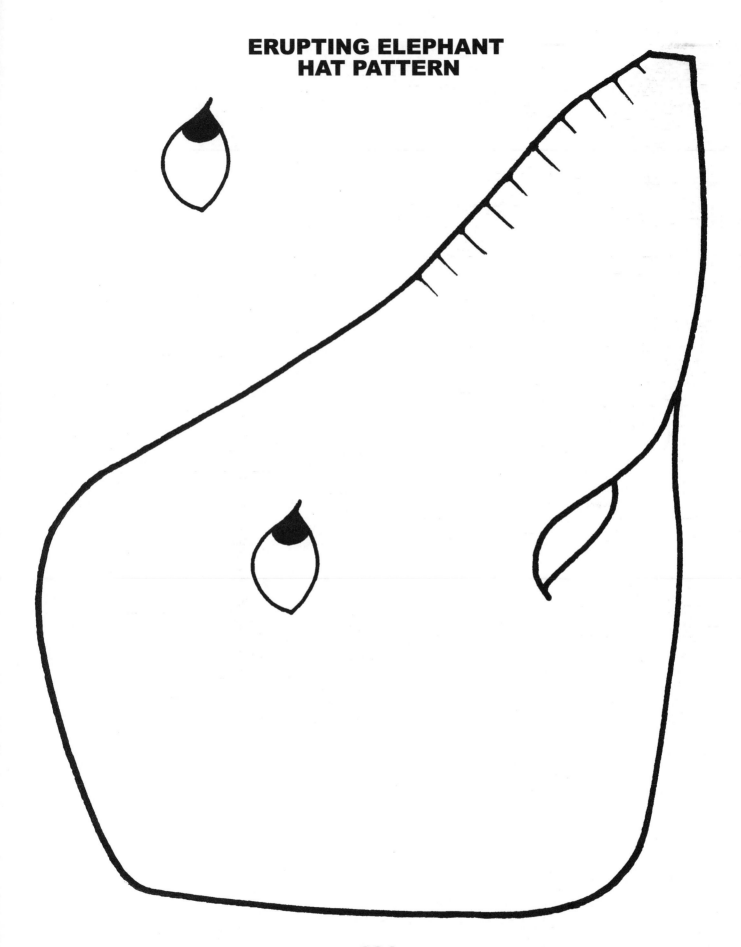

ERUPTING ELEPHANT
HAT PATTERN

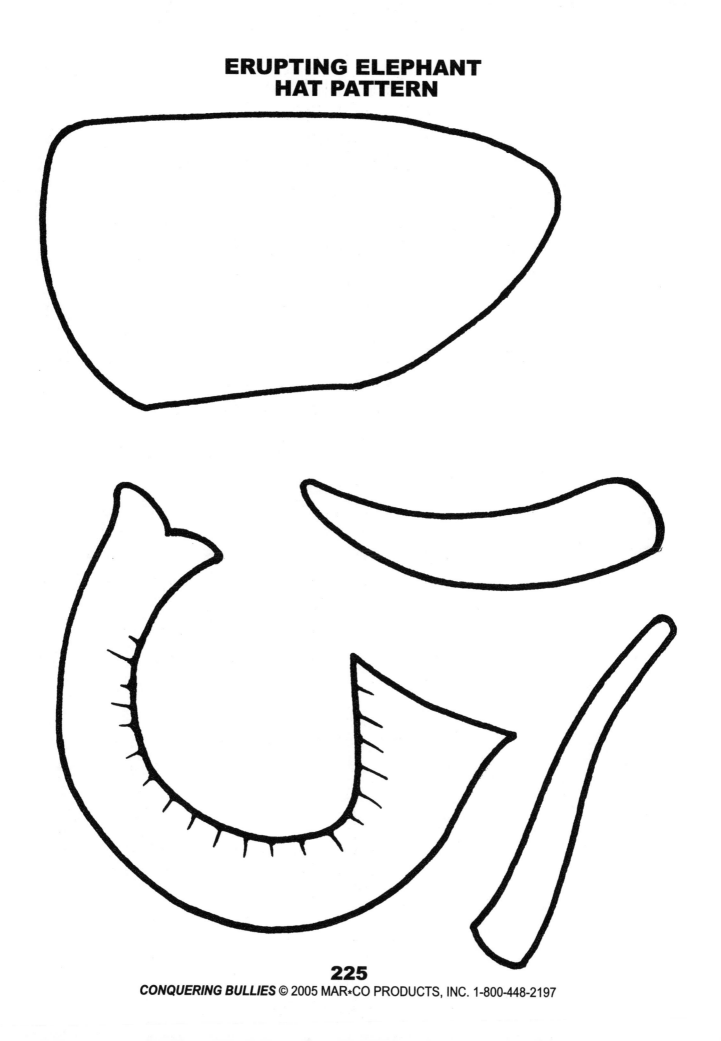

ERUPTING ELEPHANT
HAT PATTERN

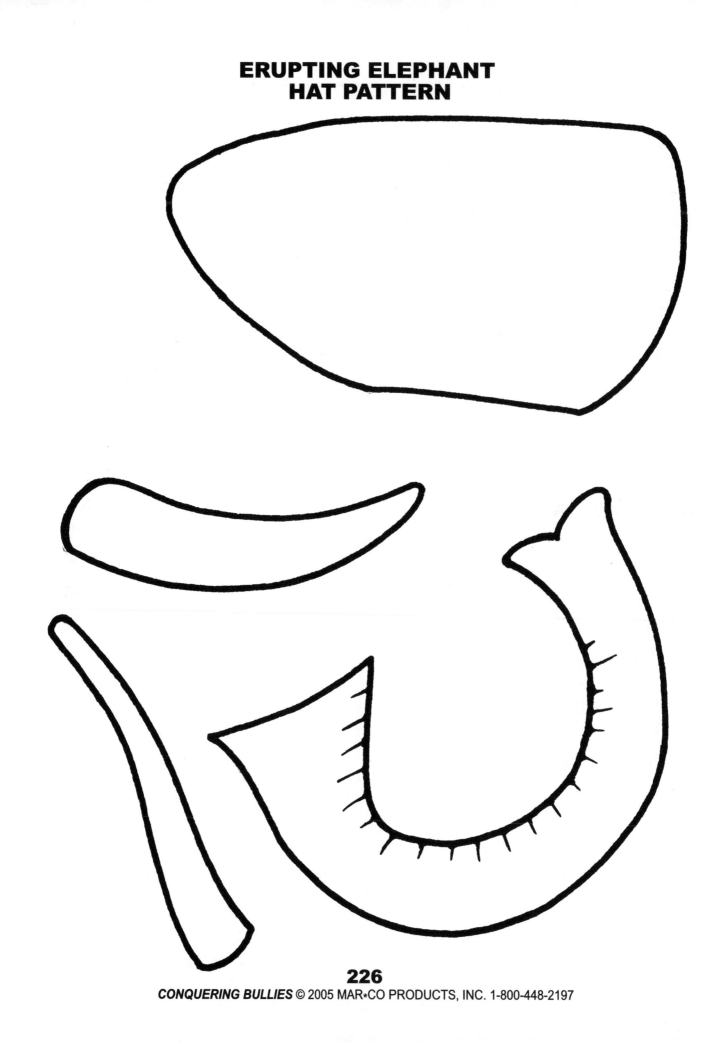

GLOATING GIRAFFE HAT

Directions:

1. Make a newspaper hat (see page 197).

2. Reproduce all the required pattern pieces on medium-weight colored paper.

   Suggested colors:

   Head: gold or tan (color the spots brown)
   Tail: gold or tan (color the spots brown)
   Horns: white
   Eyes: white

   Alternative: Reproduce the pattern pieces on medium- weight white paper and color them.

   Squiggly eyes, glitter, yarn, ribbon, etc. may also be used to decorate the hat.

3. Cut out the pattern pieces.

4. Glue the pattern pieces as shown in the above picture to both sides of the hat.

GLOATING GIRAFFE
HAT PATTERN

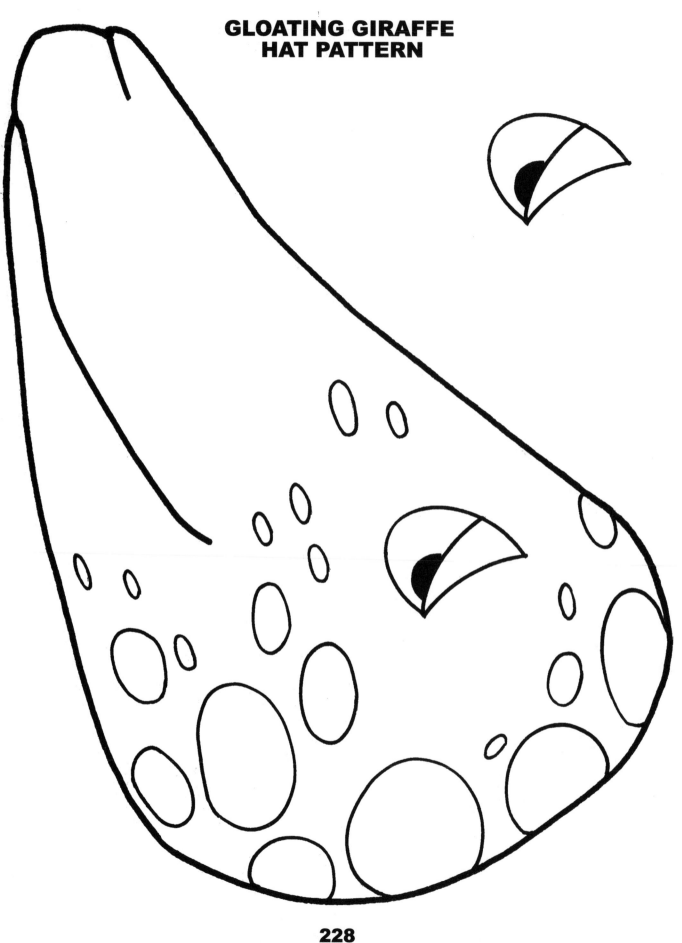

228

GLOATING GIRAFFE
HAT PATTERN

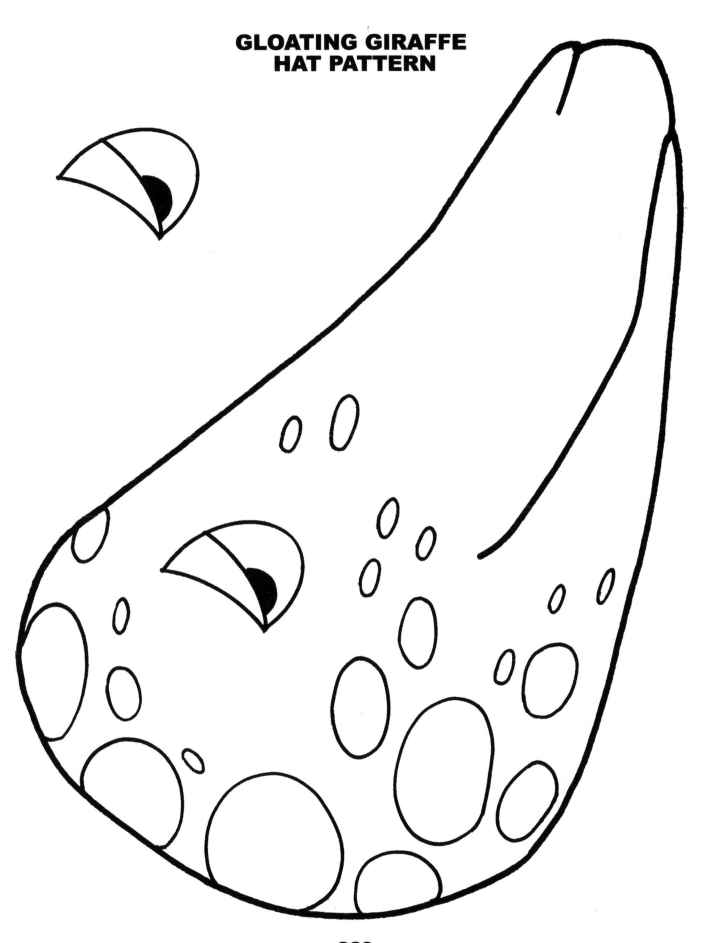

229

GLOATING GIRAFFE
HAT PATTERN

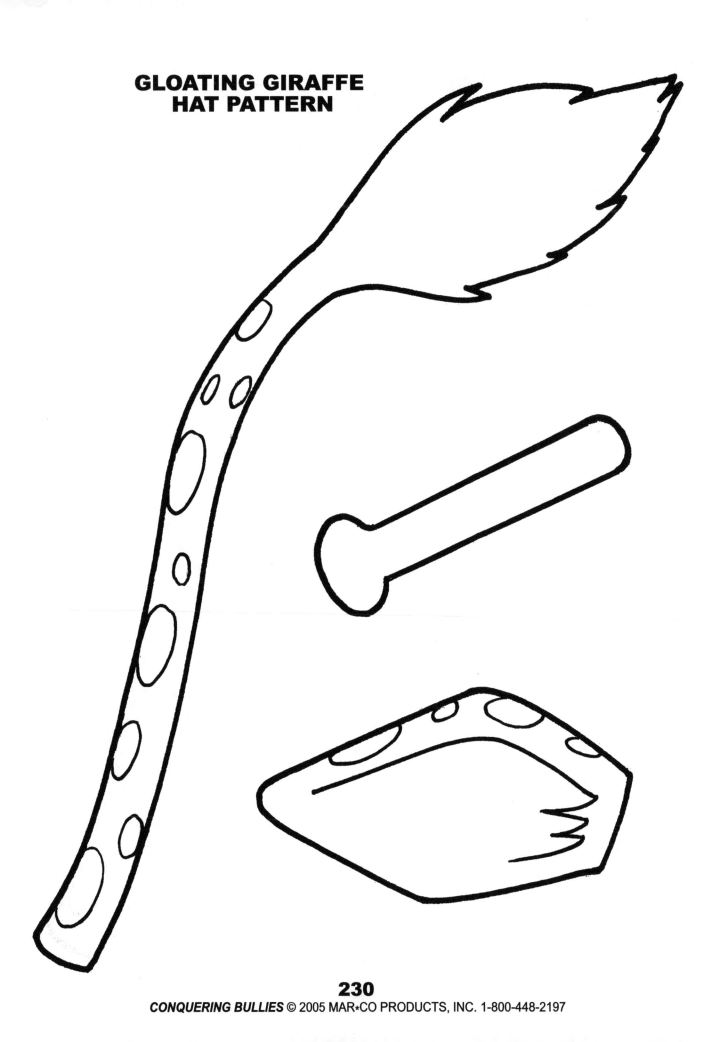

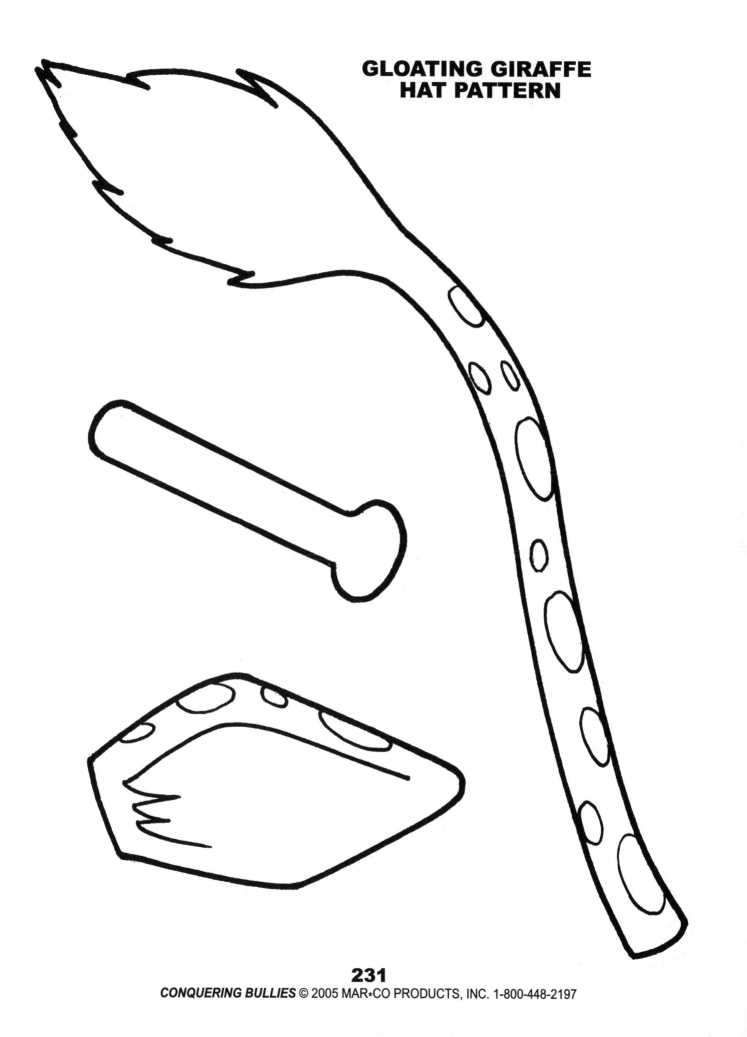

**GLOATING GIRAFFE
HAT PATTERN**

MENACING MONKEY HAT

Directions:

1. Make a newspaper hat (see page 197).

2. Reproduce all the required pattern pieces on medium-weight colored paper.

   Suggested colors:

   Head: brown or tan
   Tail: brown or tan
   Ears: brown, tan, or pink
   Eyes: white

   Alternative: Reproduce the pattern pieces on medium- weight white paper and color them.

   Squiggly eyes, glitter, yarn, ribbon, etc. may also be used to decorate the hat.

3. Cut out the pattern pieces.

4. Glue the pattern pieces as shown in the above picture to both sides of the hat.

MENACING MONKEY
HAT PATTERN

MENACING MONKEY
HAT PATTERN

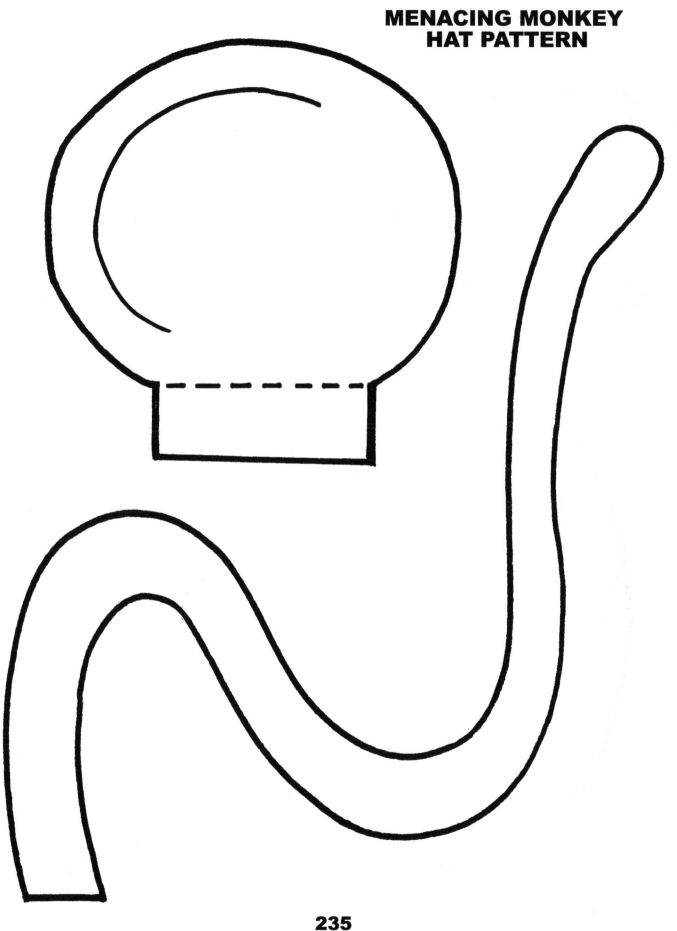

MENACING MONKEY
HAT PATTERN

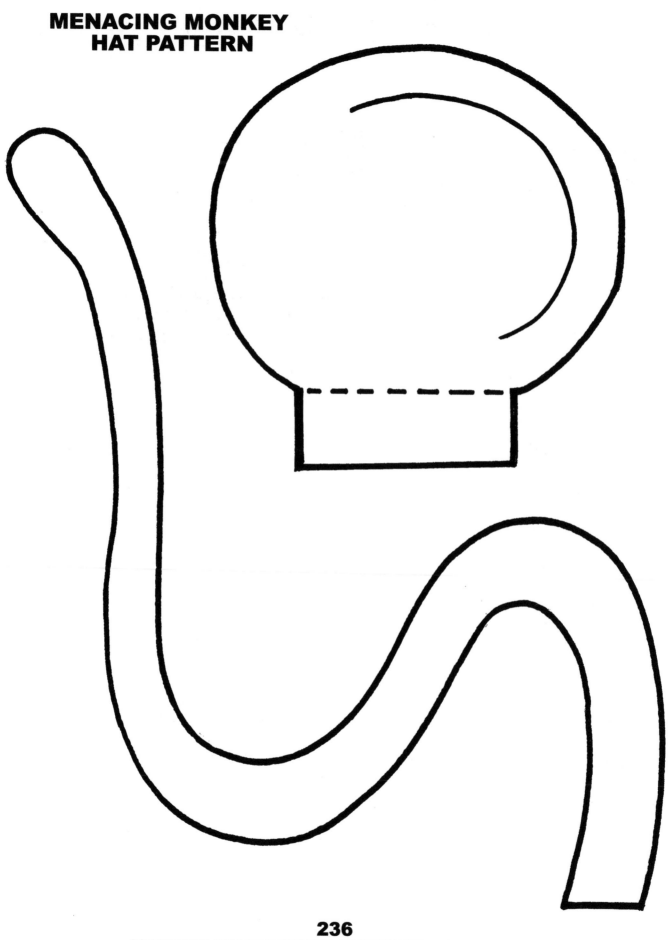

HARASSING HIPPO HAT

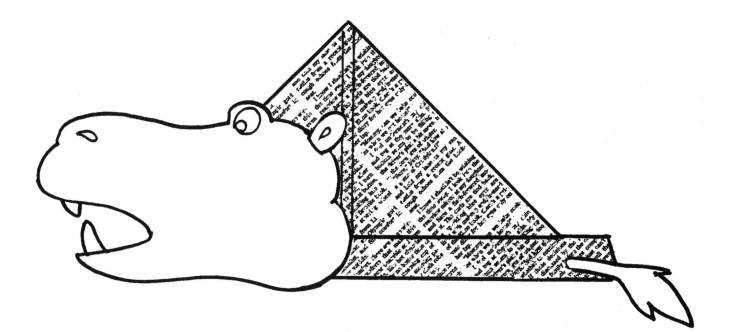

Directions:

1. Make a newspaper hat (see page 197).

2. Reproduce all the required pattern pieces on medium-weight colored paper.

   Suggested colors:

   Head: blue or purple
   Tail: blue or purple
   Eyes: white
   Teeth: white
   Ears: blue, purple, or pink

   Alternative: Reproduce the pattern pieces on medium- weight white paper and color them.

   Squiggly eyes, glitter, yarn, ribbon, etc. may also be used to decorate the hat.

3. Cut out the pattern pieces.

4. Glue the pattern pieces as shown in the above picture to both sides of the hat.

HARASSING HIPPO
HAT PATTERN

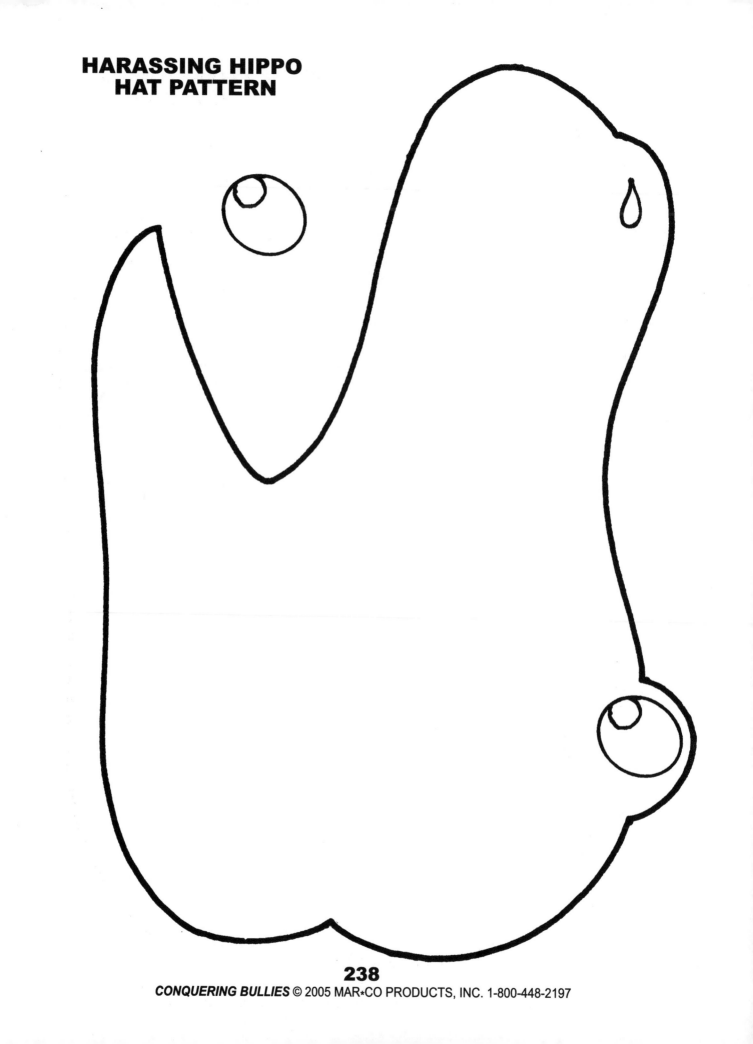

238

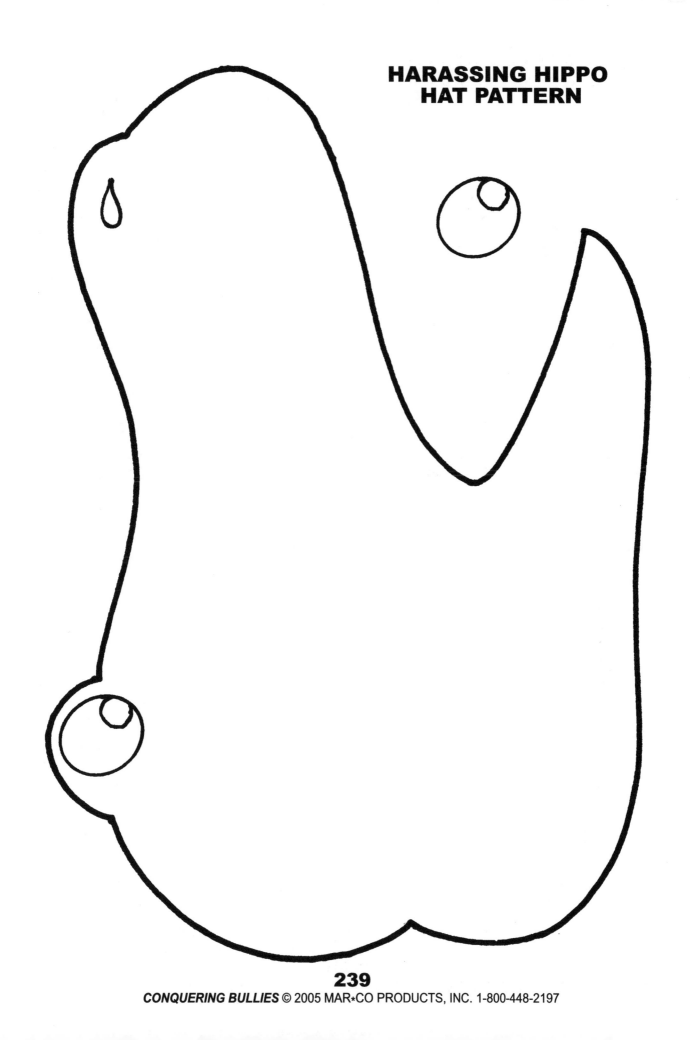

HARASSING HIPPO
HAT PATTERN

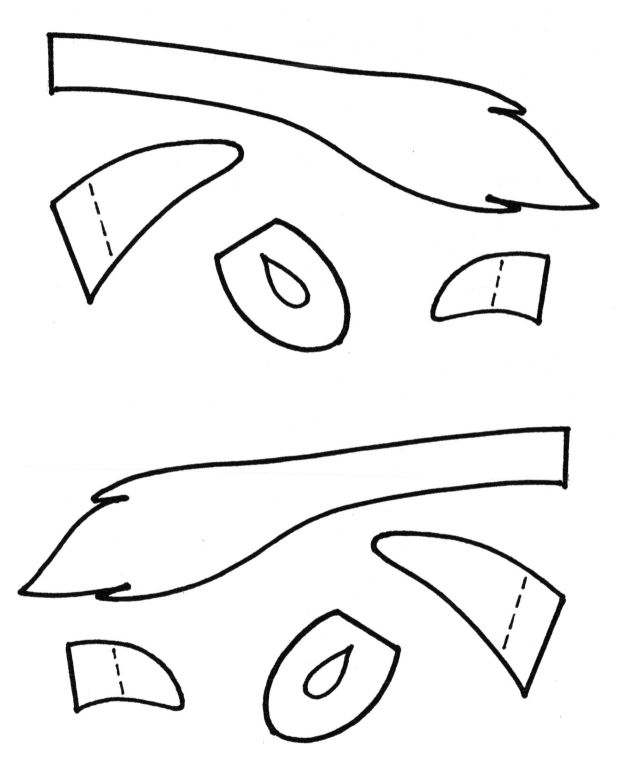

REFUSING RHINO HAT

Directions:

1. Make a newspaper hat (see page 197).

2. Reproduce all the required pattern pieces on medium-weight colored paper.

   Suggested colors:

   Head: gray or blue
   Tail: gray or blue
   Eyes: white
   Horn: white
   Ears: gray, blue, or pink

   Alternative: Reproduce the pattern pieces on medium- weight white paper and color them.

   Squiggly eyes, glitter, yarn, ribbon, etc. may also be used to decorate the hat.

3. Cut out the pattern pieces.

4. Glue the pattern pieces as shown in the above picture to both sides of the hat.

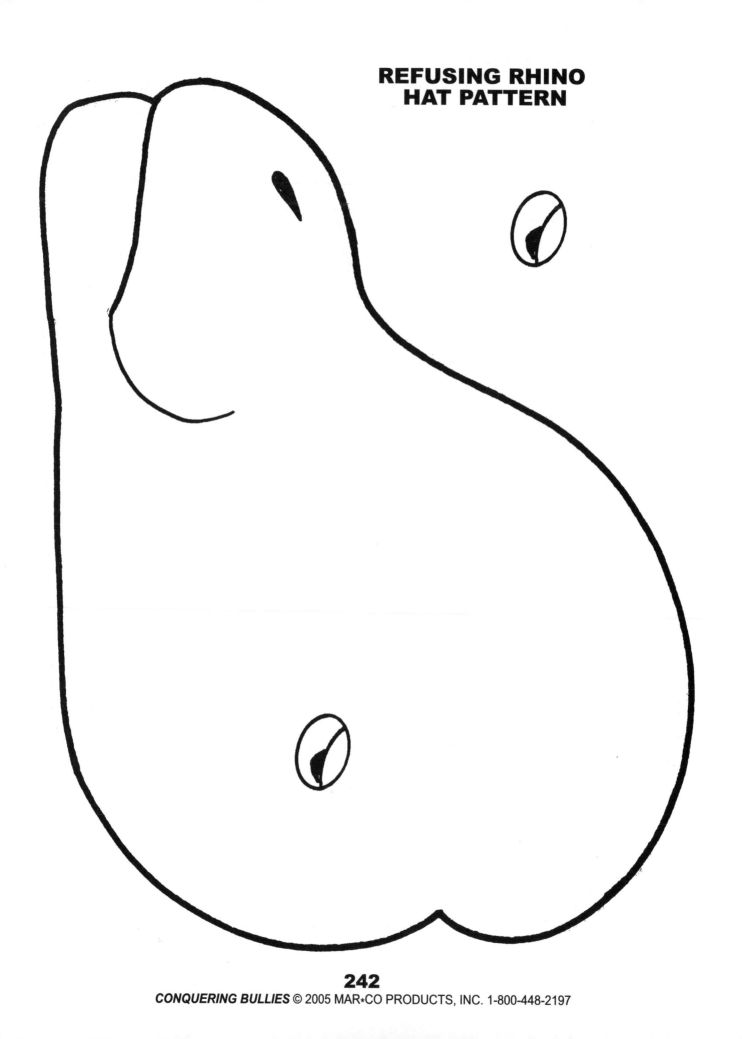

REFUSING RHINO
HAT PATTERN

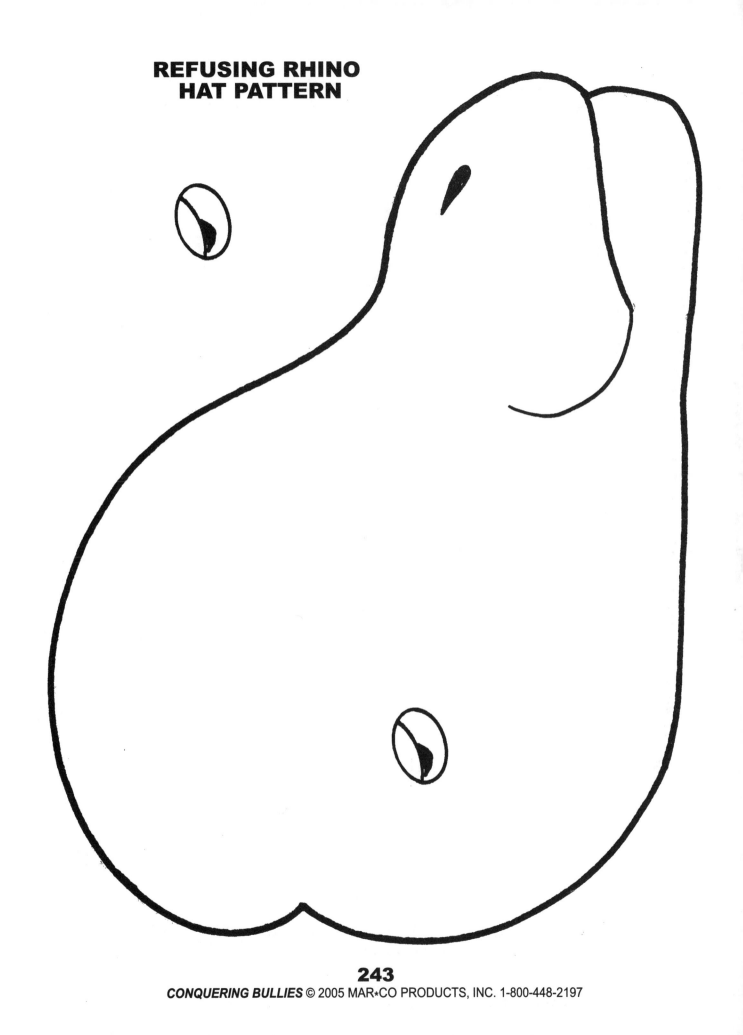

REFUSING RHINO
HAT PATTERN

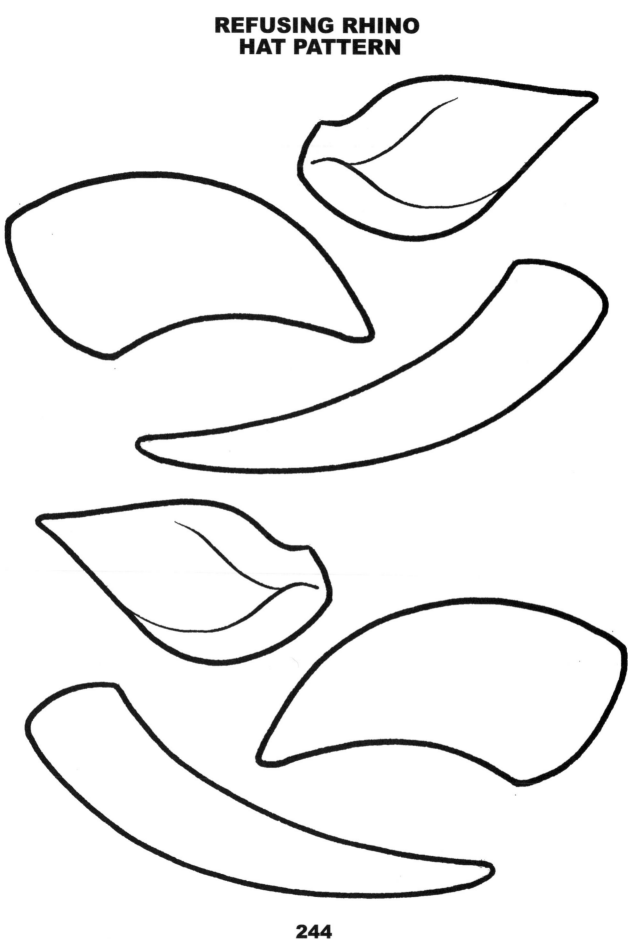

SNAPPY SNAKE HAT

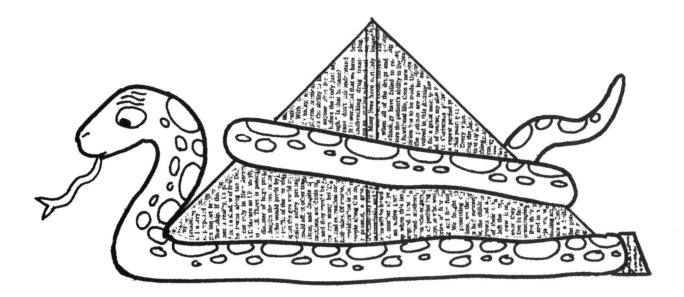

Directions:

1. Make a newspaper hat (see page 197).

2. Reproduce all the required pattern pieces on medium-weight colored paper.

   Suggested colors:

   Head and body: orange or red (color the spots purple or blue)
   Tongue: Black

   Alternative: Reproduce the pattern pieces on medium- weight white paper and color them.

   Squiggly eyes, glitter, yarn, ribbon, etc. may also be used to decorate the hat.

3. Cut out the pattern pieces.

4. Glue the pattern pieces as shown in the above picture to both sides of the hat.

SNAPPY SNAKE
HAT PATTERN

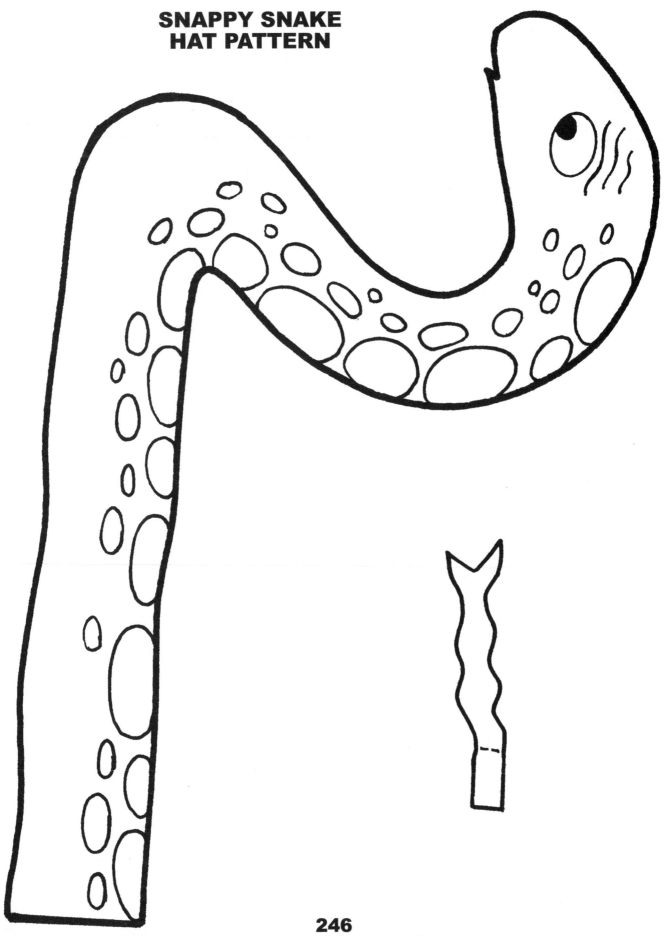

SNAPPY SNAKE
HAT PATTERN

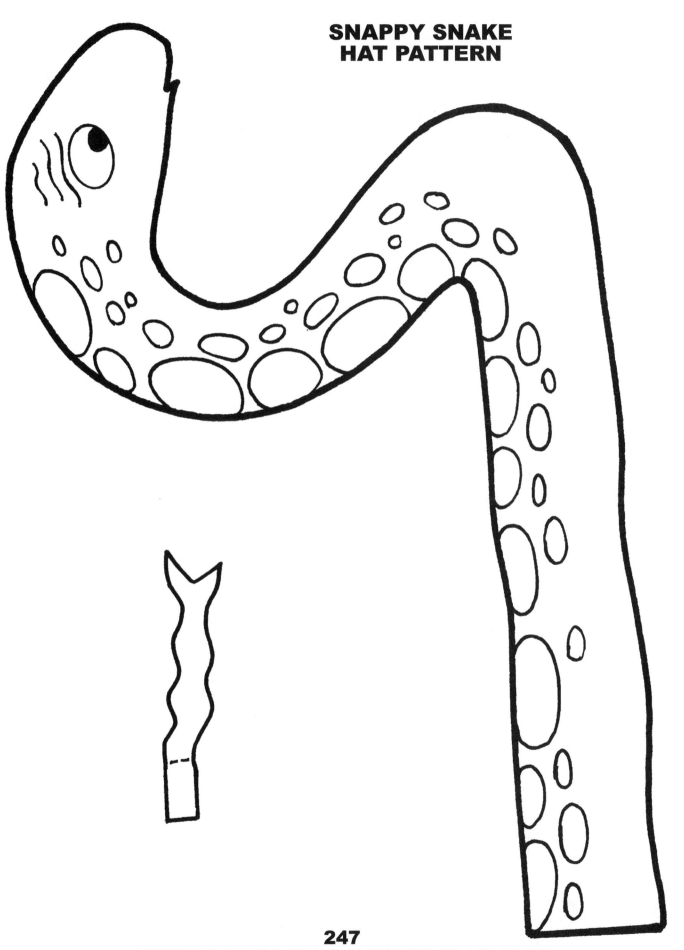

SNAPPY SNAKE
HAT PATTERN

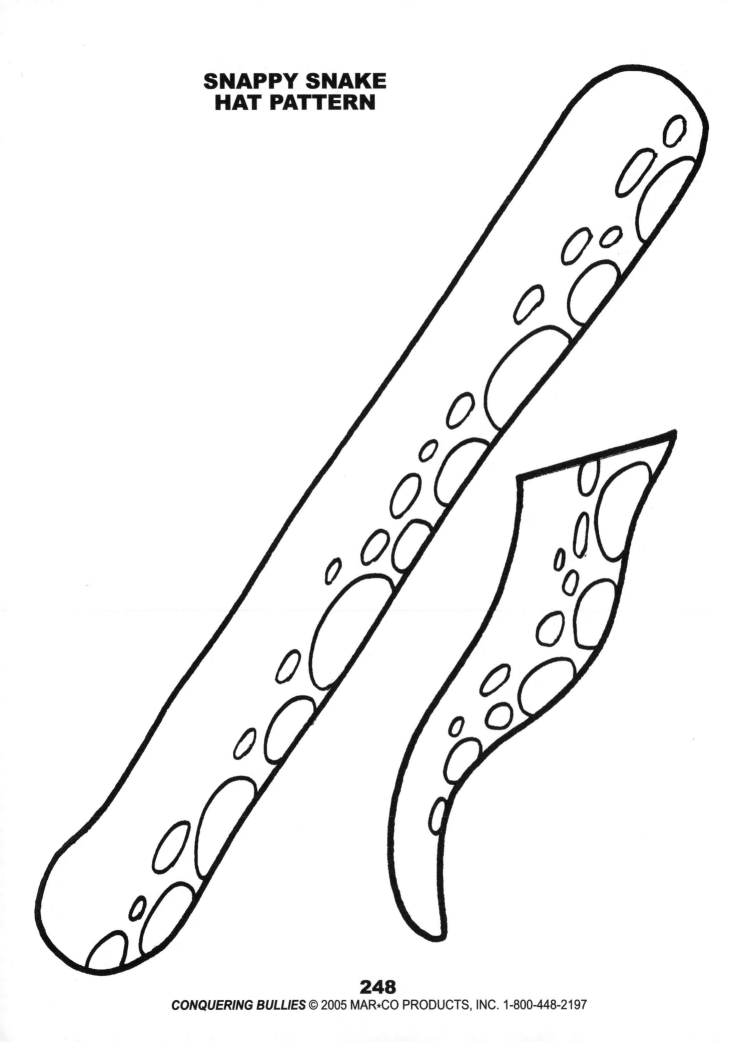

SNAPPY SNAKE
HAT PATTERN

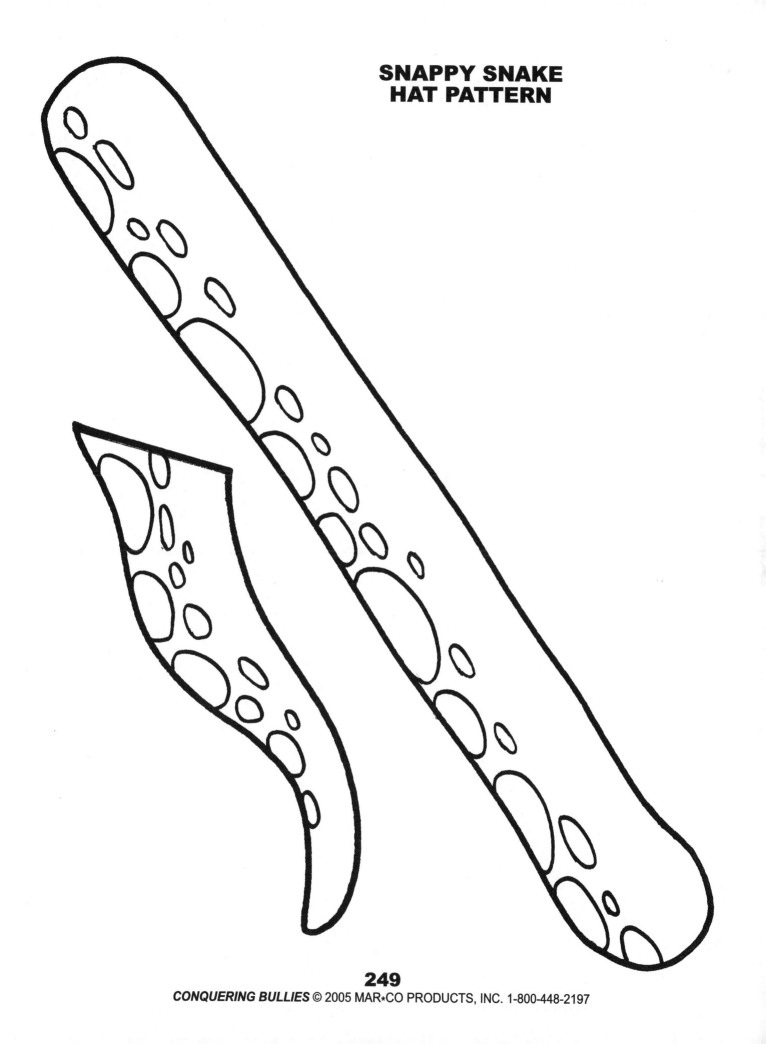

SNAPPY SNAKE
HAT PATTERN

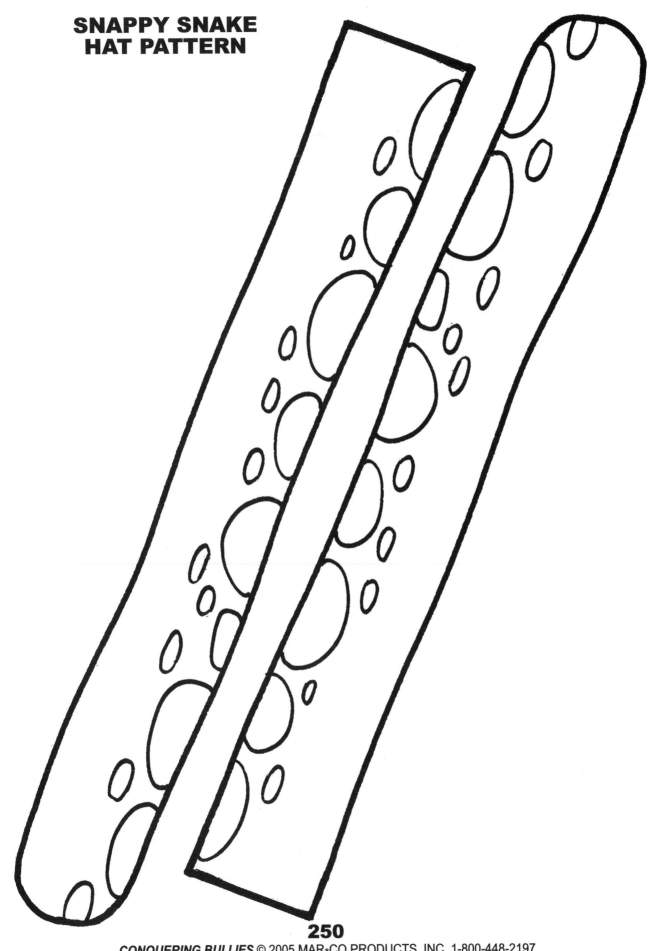

250

CROAKING CROCODILE HAT

Directions:

1. Make a newspaper hat (see page 197).

2. Reproduce all the required pattern pieces on medium-weight colored paper.

   Suggested colors:

   Head: green
   Body: green
   Tail: green
   Teeth: yellow or white
   Eyes: red or white

   Alternative: Reproduce the pattern pieces on medium- weight white paper and color them.

   Squiggly eyes, glitter, yarn, ribbon, etc. may also be used to decorate the hat.

3. Cut out the pattern pieces.

4. Glue the pattern pieces as shown in the above picture to both sides of the hat.

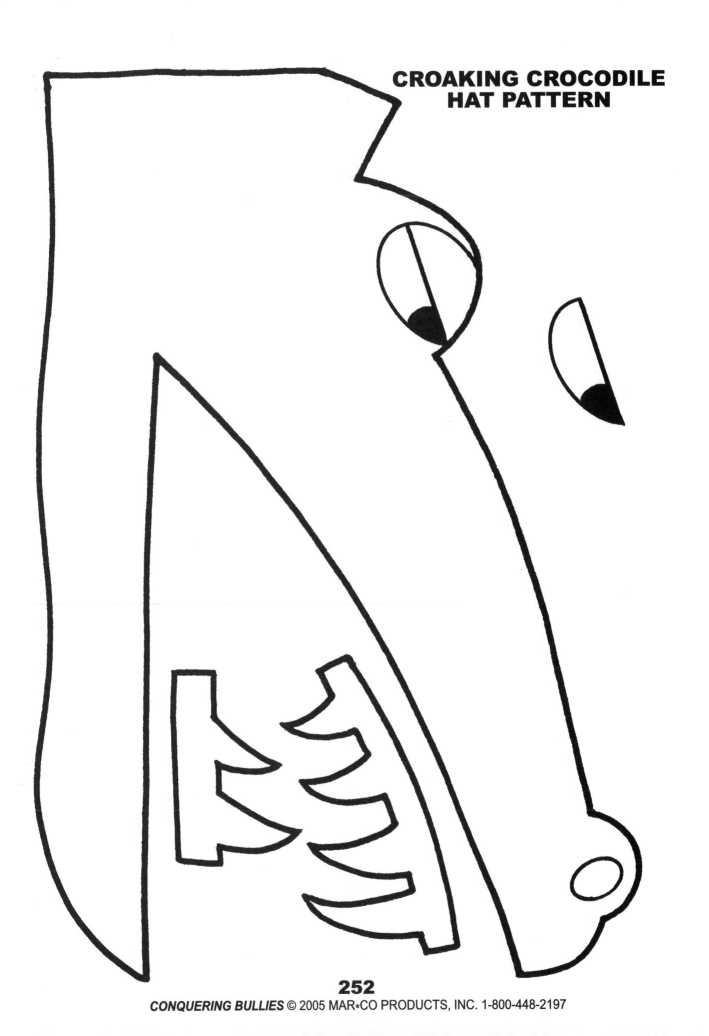

CROAKING CROCODILE
HAT PATTERN

CONQUERING BULLIES © 2005 MAR*CO PRODUCTS, INC. 1-800-448-2197

CROAKING CROCODILE
HAT PATTERN

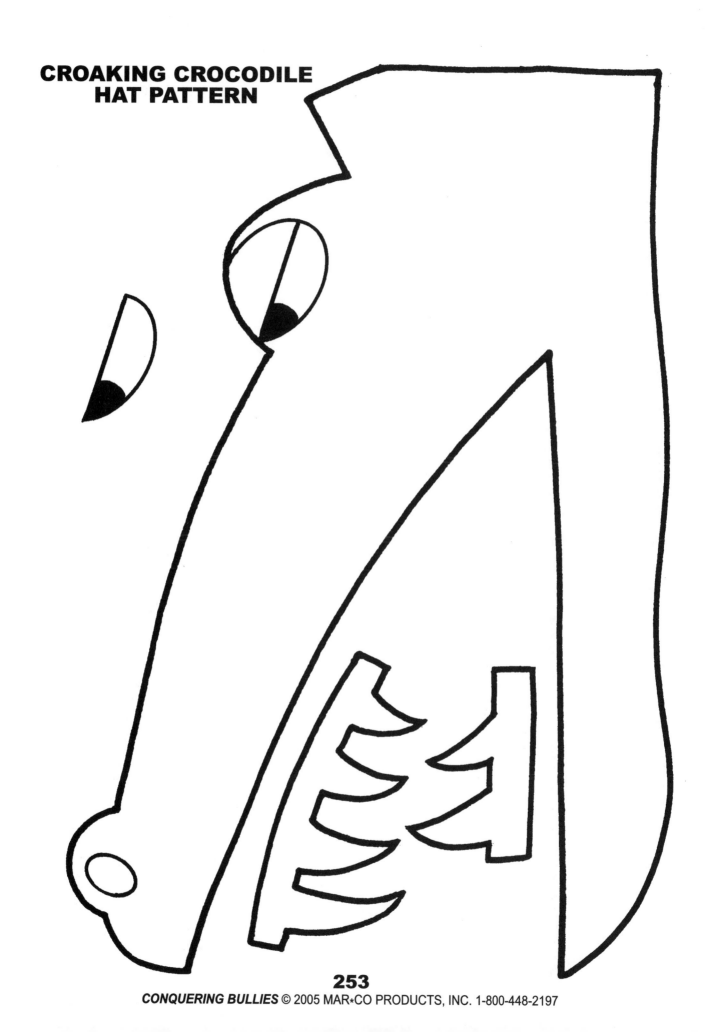

253

CROAKING CROCODILE
HAT PATTERN

CROAKING CROCODILE
HAT PATTERN

Marianne Vandawalker

Marianne is a recently retired counselor from North Carolina. She holds a MED and certifications in reading and Language Arts. She has worked as a special reading teacher as well as a classroom instructor of courses ranging from Head Start to high school English.

Marianne reaches students with high-interest material and activities. It is her goal to meet the counseling needs of young people of various ages. She accomplishes this through active classroom guidance, which raises awareness and skills, and works to improve skills in small-group settings. Used each day, her lessons enhance the performance of students and teachers alike. Repetition results in changes and improvements.

Other Books By Marianne Vandawalker Available From
MAR*CO PRODUCTS, INC.

Character Fun Game Kit

Career Fun Game Kit

Study Skills Fun Game Kit

Career Pay Day